FENG SHUI
ASTROLOGY

D1375552

FENG SHUI ASTROLOGY

USING 9 STAR KI TO ACHIEVE HARMONY
& HAPPINESS IN YOUR LIFE

JON SANDIFER
FOREWORD BY WILLIAM SPEAR

PIATKUS

For my children:

Justin
James
Chloë
Josh
Luke
Chiara

© 1997 Jon Sandifer

First published in 1997 by
Judy Piatkus (Publishers) Ltd
5 Windmill Street, London W1P 1HF

Reprinted 1998

**The moral right of the author
has been asserted**

*A catalogue record for this book is available
from the British Library*

ISBN 0–7499–1709–1 pbk

Edited by Esther Jagger
Designed by Sue Ryall
Artwork by Zena Flax

Data capture & manipulation by
Phoenix Photosetting, Chatham, Kent
Printed & bound in Great Britain by
Biddles Ltd, Guildford & King's Lynn

CONTENTS

ACKNOWLEDGEMENTS

To Michio Kushi, for the first contact I had with 9 Star Ki astrology in 1977 at an evening lecture at the East-West Centre, London. I still have my first notes, scribbled on the back of old envelopes!

To Rex Lasalle, my first Shiatsu teacher who shared the same enthusiasm for 9 Star Ki and who gave me my first and treasured copy of *An Anthology of I Ching*.

To friends and colleagues for their insights, wisdom, books, publications and especially the late night discussions on the subject – Bob Sachs, Steve Gagné, Martin Halsey, Ed Esko, Denny Waxman and Lenny Jacobs.

To William Spear for his friendship, encouragement and inspiration these past twenty years.

To Takashi Yoshikawa, forty-five years a world authority on this subject, whom I had the honour to meet in 1994 and 1995.

To Gina Lazenby for the trust and support she has given me in promoting my workshops.

To Anne Lawrance at Piatkus for having the foresight to see the potential of this book and for making it possible.

To all my clients and participants in seminars over the years who make this study real and practical.

To all my family for giving me the time and space to create and complete this book.

Thank you all.

FOREWORD

The world is changing faster than ever. Or is it? People are not the same as they used to be. Or are they? The secrets of the sages are complex, subtle, deep. Or maybe they're simple. Have we forgotten the most basic qualities of human design – our fullest potential inherent at birth - assuming this information is too specialised for us mere mortals?

What is it that truly connects us all? And what would life be like if we were unaware of the complete picture, of history, planning our future through guesswork without the benefit of knowledge, systems, principles, information?

My idea of hell is a place where nothing connects.
T. S. Eliot

Imagine . . . A surgeon walks into the operating theatre. He takes a scalpel and makes an incision. The patient's pulse quickens, blood pressure dropping, as an assistant speaks. 'Doctor, would you like to review the patient's profile before continuing?' Unaware of the possibilities of modern technology, the startled medicine man looks up. 'What kind of information do you have?' Others in the room look on in amazement. 'Well, Doctor, we have x-rays and a scan.' After a moment of reflection, the red-faced professional blurts out, 'No, I'll just do the best I can.' You could hear a pin drop.

Imagine . . . A salesman – an amateur pilot – arrives at the airport where he keeps his small, single engine aircraft. 'A beautiful day for a joy ride', he announces as he walks directly to his plane. He starts the engine, taxis to the nearest runway and then takes off into the sky. Air traffic control watches in disbelief, trying in vain to reach him by radio. 'A beautiful day . . .' he repeats as he climbs higher, narrowly missing an incoming jetliner making its final approach . . .

Imagine . . . The sales director of a large computer company meets a potential client, a Mr Ahashi, for dinner at a small Japanese restaurant. A successful meeting could double her income. Once seated, she is handed a menu written in the characters of an alphabet she cannot understand. She crosses her fingers and points at random to a dish. Pretending to be in perfect control, she remains poker-faced as a platter of raw octopus is placed in front of her . . .

Every professional has a training, a language, a set of skills and reference points that make it possible to do the job well. But excellence is not something that just arrives; it is developed over time, built upon experience, knowledge, understanding and wisdom. Just as we begin to reach this level, retirement and pensions loom on the horizon.

It would be wonderful if our children each arrived with an instruction book that could help us to serve their needs. But every parent has to learn from practice, patience and the counsel of elders. By the time we begin to get an idea of what we're really doing, our children are planning their own families!

Imagine . . . A system that delivers an entirely new perspective on the one thing most of us never master: time. A philosophy tried and tested since human civilisation began. A teaching so elegant, so practical and universal that virtually every doctor (after reviewing the patient's medical history), every pilot (after checking with air traffic control), every corporate executive (after studying the language and customs of the marketplace) and – oh, yes – even every parent can benefit by applying its basic principles in daily life. All of this is now offered by a master teacher, a father and a healer who is willing to share his 20 years of experience.

This volume – full of possibility, insight and practical guidance – will firmly establish the incalculable value of Feng Shui in our lives. You will be changed forever by its wisdom.

Using what you read here will surely bring you good luck. May it also provide you with the most fortunate blessings!

William Spear
On a beautiful spring day in London, 1997

INTRODUCTION

Probably the oldest form of astrology, 9 Star Ki astrology originated in early Chinese civilisation where it was known as Chiu Kung Ming Li. It has been refined throughout the centuries and in the past forty years has enjoyed increased popularity in Japan and the Western world.

Almost all early civilisations looked towards the heavens for guidance and inspiration. Our forbears understood intuitively that life on our earth was influenced by the seasons and the climate of the universe. Throughout the ancient world there was a fundamental understanding of 'energy', known to the Japanese as Ki, to the Chinese as Chi, to the Hindus as Prana and to the ancient Egyptians as Kaa. This energy was seen to have two basic natures. Firstly there was the energy that emanated from the earth, which gave rise to landscape, water and the soil. Secondly there was the energy of 'heaven' or 'infinity', which was seen to determine our seasons and our climate. Variations within these cycles were believed to influence the year in which we were born and the year that we were currently occupying.

Ancient peoples felt that the universal Ki energy, originating deep in the cosmos, was filtered primarily by nine stars – hence 9 Star Ki.

The outer limits of this filter or funnel were seen as the two stars Vega and Polaris. Vega represented one end of the

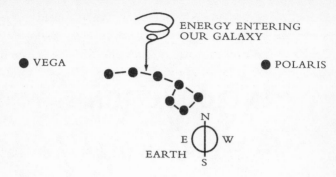

Ancient peoples believed that Ki energy was filtered by nine stars

spectrum: cold, winter and the passive energy of the moon. Polaris, on the other hand, was associated with the sun and the active energies of fire. Vega and Polaris were also linked, respectively, with the forces known as yin and yang (see Chapter 1). Between these two stars lie the seven stars of the Ursa Major constellation, also known as the Great Bear or Great Dipper. Essentially, the Ursa Major constellation rotates between Polaris and Vega and in ancient times acted as a compass pointing out a different direction in each season (see diagram above). This understanding gave rise to the idea of the seasonal nature of cosmic energy as it approached the earth. This is the basis of 9 Star Ki astrology and will be developed later.

Feng Shui

Around the world, civilisations modern and ancient have appreciated the qualities of Ki energy in their environment. Traditionally, the application of this understanding was pure common sense. You would build your home or village away from damp places with poor soil, you would work out the place where the sun shone best, and you would avoid areas where former inhabitants had suffered from chronic illness or been unable to grow crops. In the same way, ancient peoples appreciated that they could build their homes and villages in such a way as to optimise self-protection, health and communications. As Feng Shui developed over the centuries, it became more mathematical and scientific.

Feng Shui and 9 Star Ki Astrology

These systems have one major common denominator – they both draw aspects of their understanding from an ancient text called the *I Ching* or *Book of Changes* (see Chapter 3). The *I Ching* is one of the earliest forms of divination, and draws strongly on the premise that the actions of humanity are the results of the action of the complementary forces of yin and yang (see Chapter 1).

Nine Star Ki astrology developed out of the same stable as Feng Shui, traditional Chinese medicine and acupuncture. Feng Shui deals primarily with space, whereas 9 Star Ki astrology is devoted to understanding time. There are a number of forms of oriental astrology, and the Compass School of Feng Shui links Feng Shui and astrology. However, 9 Star Ki astrology does not sit within one particular 'school' of Feng Shui but rather brings another perspective to Feng Shui, using the same original principles.

What 9 Star Ki Astrology Can Offer You

Chapters 1, 2 and 3 will provide a background to the nature of traditional oriental philosophy by explaining the basics of the *I Ching*, yin and yang and the Five Transformations. These areas lead into the three most important aspects of 9 Star Ki astrology.

Who you are

Apart from the nine stars already mentioned, this system of astrology is also based on the influence of a perceived nine-year cycle (and within that, monthly, daily and hourly cycles). You will discover from this book which 'star' was present in your year of birth and influences your principal nature. In Chapter 2 you will find out how to calculate your principal number, which could be regarded as similar to the Sun sign in Western astrology. (This number is also sometimes referred to as your constitutional number). The information in Chapter 4 forms the basis of who you are, what your potential is and how you will relate to the other eight stars. These relationships are presented in Chapter 5, which offers fascinating insights into who you are and how you relate to others in your family, at work and in social situations.

In Chapter 7 you take a deeper look at your character. Given that this is an astrology based on nine-year and nine-month cycles, your character number is drawn from your month of birth and is similar to the Moon sign in Western astrology. The influence of this star in your chart gives you an insight into your driving force and nature.

In Chapter 8 you will discover your energetic number. This is expressed in the way you appear to others, go about your tasks and express yourself. In Western astrology this is known as your ascendant or rising sign.

These three numbers combine to give a unique perspective on who you are. The nine years and nine months give a potential 81 combinations of these numbers which are presented in Chapter 9, along with contemporary and historical figures who share your chart.

In completing 'who' you are, Chapter 10 looks at your sexuality relative to your astrological chart drawn from 9 Star Ki. To make the most of this chapter you must first familiarise yourself with Chapters 1-5.

Where you are

Chapters 6, 11 and 12 deal with where you are during the nine year cycle. This cycle could be regarded as similar to our familiar four seasons. During these nine yearly cycles there will be times when you pass through a winter 'phase' – you feel dormant, quiet and less sociable, which is not necessarily a good time to initiate new projects or major changes. In another phase of the nine year cycle you will pass through 'autumn' – good for stabilising and harvesting your effort – or a 'spring' phase when you have your greatest opportunity for growth and new beginnings. In 9 Star Ki each of these phases is known as a 'house'. Knowing where you are, i.e. which house you are currently occupying, within this cycle of nine years can be of immense value if you are considering moving house, changing your job or initiating a new project. Chapter 12 looks specifically at the underlying nine month cycle that co-exists with the yearly cycle. Where you are within the cycle of nine months affects your health, your emotions and your communication with others.

Directionology

Chapter 13 will enable you to choose the best directions for moving house, changing job or office location, or taking a holiday. The information is all based on the previous principles that relate to who you are and where you are, and examples are given of directions that others have taken to their benefit or disadvantage.

Since first coming across 9 Star Ki in 1977, I have discovered that it is well worth pursuing. I not only value the accuracy of the system, but I am also excited by its inherent simplicity. There is a little arithmetic involved; I am no mathematician, but I have found no problems in understanding 9 Star Ki. Just double check your calculations to begin with, and very soon the process will become second nature.

I enjoy sailing – the freedom, the open sea, the fresh air and the adventure. However, this romantic notion can only be realised with the benefit of good navigation. With poor navigation I have experienced worry, danger and discomfort, and frequently wished I was back at home. But with good navigation – going with the Ki, taking into account the winds, the tide and my location – I felt invigorated and satisfied with the outcome. I invite you too to use 9 Star Ki astrology as an invaluable navigational tool in our changing and often tempestuous world.

1

YIN AND YANG

Complementary Opposites

If you study any aspect of oriental philosophy or culture you soon come across the terms 'yin' and 'yang'. These terms are used to describe the opposite yet complementary nature of Ki energy which ancient people understood to be present behind the manifestation of anything in nature – the creation of structures, actions, seasons, emotions and movement.

In 9 Star Ki astrology the qualities of yin and yang lie behind the understanding of the cycles of change that we go through. These nine-year cycles, which you will study in Chapter 11, are moving from yin to yang; this means from dormancy in winter (yin) through the active rising stage of

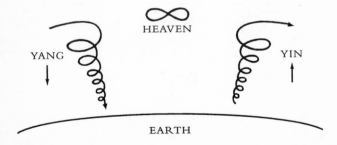

Yang energy emanates from the heavens, yin energy rises from the earth

spring to the consolidation stages of yang. Similarly, the principal numbers also contain yin/yang attributes.

Yang's nature is seen to emanate from the heavens and descend towards the earth (see p. 7). Conversely, yin's natural tendency is to rise and return towards the heavens. As yin's energy rises it becomes more diffused, and therefore slower and cooler, whereas yang's descending energy becomes more concentrated, harder, hotter and faster. The outcome of this process is that structures that are bigger are seen as more yin, while those that are smaller and more compact are seen as more yang. Here is a list of some typical opposites associated with yin and yang.

Yang	Yin
activity	passivity
heat	coolness
movement	stillness
power (obvious)	potential energy (power)
confident	self-conscious
passionate	cool
extrovert	introvert
impulsive	diligent
stubborn	flexible
bold	cautious
paternal	maternal
adventurous	insecure
independent	dependent

Intermingled Concepts

An important principle to bear in mind is that nothing is totally yin and nothing is totally yang. The following centuries-old symbol expresses this concept perfectly. The dark section on the left is representative of yang, but within it is

The yin yang symbol

a small circle of the opposite (yin) from the right-hand side. If we were to look at a tree we could say that its leaves, branches and trunk represent the yin element in its structure and that the yang expression is within its downward-growing roots. A spring onion has far more upward nature (yin) within its structure and far less root (yang); compare this with a carrot, which has a greater concentration of energy and structure within its root (yang) and less emphasis on the leaf structure (yin).

Similarly, if our nature is predominantly spiritual or intellectual we are more yin than an individual who is practical and grounded, who would be seen as more yang. People who are physically and emotionally flexible would be relatively more yin than people who are more rigid and inflexible. Night-time, when we rest and are more passive, is traditionally understood as a more yin time, whereas the daylight hours when we are active and busy are seen as more yang. Winter, when it is colder and we are less active, is more yin than the summertime, when it is hotter and we are more outdoor and active. However, during the winter, when we are passive and nature seems equally inactive, a process of yangisation is occurring. We tend to reflect on and consolidate our achievements and successes at this time. During the night, when we are asleep, we are also revitalising ourselves and conserving our energy to face the tasks of the next day. These are just a few examples of nothing being totally yin or yang.

In ancient times people learnt from their surroundings in the natural world. It is therefore not surprising that they described the qualities of yin and yang from nature, the elements and the seasons. To avoid the danger of categorising all that we see into lists of yin and yang, let's take a closer look at nature in terms of yin and yang.

Wood

Structures built of light, hollow, flexible types of wood have an uplifting nature but at the same time a lack of stability. If you were chairing an important meeting you would appreciate a strong, solid oak chair to support you, but you might feel less confident in a flimsy bamboo beach chair. The latter, however, would be ideal if you were on holiday and wanted to relax with an informal routine. The more solid timbers that take time to grow and mature, such as oak, are far more yang than the hollow, lighter structures of bamboo that only take weeks to grow.

Rocks

Almost all mineral structures in nature needed time, pressure and heat to form. The more of these qualities that were present, the more yang the structure of the resultant rocks. One of the most yang geological structures is granite, which took unimaginable time and pressure to form and can withstand the battering of the elements for thousands of years. Younger, sedimentary rocks exhibit far less yang. Equally, while the granite may be a fine example of yang energy it does not allow much yin expression to be present. This is seen in the lack of vegetation, the dryness and the absence of the freshness and vitality that you can feel when you walk on lighter or more sandy mineral structures.

Soils

Clay is a great example of a yang soil structure, heavy, sticky and rich in minerals. It can be made even more yang by the use of fire. Compost, light soil and sand are examples of yin soil structures which, although fertile, tend to be superficial and easily eroded by rain.

Fire

A fire made from twigs or leaves or paper may appear superficially bright and roaring, but it does not have the yang to sustain long, slow combustion. Compare this with a fire of coal or charcoal, which will burn steadily for hours at a constant temperature – it is easy to see that the slower fire is more yang. It is not its superficial quality that merits this description but its inner nature.

Water

This element provides a whole spectrum of yin/yang qualities. Fresh, clear, running water that can appear superficially yang (because it is active) is really presenting us with some of the finest qualities of yin: its freshness and vitality represent yin's 'upward' nature. Conversely, the stillness and depth of water that we perceive in a lake or an ocean may appear superficially yin (inactive), but its hidden strength and deeper nature are the clue to its more yang nature.

Activities

Pursuits that we engage in that are practical and 'hands-on' are regarded as more yang, whereas reading, writing, inventing and discussion are all seen as more yin activities. Being led is more yin than being the leader. Working in a group as part of a team is more yin, while working alone and in isolation is more yang. Lazing in the sun on a tropical beach is definitely yin compared to climbing a mountain in the Alps alone which is yang.

Health

Yin symptoms

Tiredness is a common problem in modern life and is a good example of a yin symptom. Its causes can be lack of fresh air, over-eating, not enough sleep or not enough variety in our lives. Feeling withdrawn and fearful while at the same time avoiding engaging in too much activity is another yin symptom. Craving sweet foods, sweet drinks, ice cream, chocolate and stimulants such as coffee is also symptomatic of a yin condition. A very practical way of assessing your condition is to see whether your hands are damp or dry: any excess damp is yin.

Yang symptoms

Being hyperactive – unable to rest, to slow down or even have a full night's sleep – is a symptom of an over-yang condition. If you crave salty, savoury or hot foods and like plenty of physical activity for recreation then your condition is more yang. Dry hands with a firm handshake is another sign of a yang condition.

2

THE FIVE
TRANSFORMATIONS

Yin and yang is the dynamic that underpins the oriental arts and sciences, and it was further developed in the field of healing. In traditional Chinese medicine yin and yang gave a practitioner the basic tools for diagnosis. About 2600 BC the Yellow Emperor wrote a classic work called the *Nei Ching*, the original treatise on Chinese medicine. In it he introduced a deeper view of yin and yang that includes stages of change or transformations that occur throughout a cycle.

It is these transformational stages that form the basis of the nine principal numbers that are associated with the characters in 9 Star Ki astrology. Where and how did this system evolve from yin and yang?

How the Transformations Came About

As you can see from the diagram overleaf, the upward cycle of energy on the left represents yin's nature (rising) whereas the downward side of the cycle on the right represents yang's nature (descending).

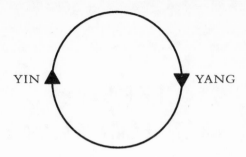

This cycle was later divided into four clear stages which can be seen in the following diagram.

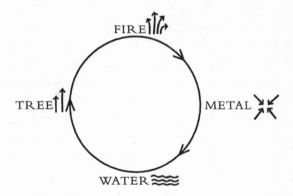

The rising side of the cycle was given the element Tree, while the upper and outward growing part of the cycle was given the element Fire. The descending quarter of the cycle was given the contracting element of Metal, and finally the lower and still portion of the cycle was given the natural element Water.

Although these stages could be regarded as representing the four seasons (Tree = spring, Fire = summer, Metal = autumn, Water = winter), there was seen to be a fifth stage that was pivotal to all the stages or seasons. This was given a unique position at the centre of the cycle (see the following diagram) and is known as Soil. As each season/transformation moved into the next, it passed through the Soil stage.

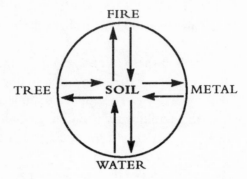

This Soil season was understood to be that unclear phase between seasons when the weather and climate could easily revert to the previous season for a few days and then advance to the next for a few days. We are all familiar with this turning point when we are not sure, for instance, whether it is spring or summer yet. Finally, Soil was given its own place within the cycle between Fire and Metal.

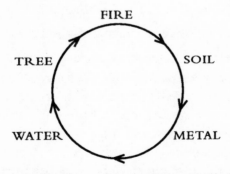

These stages of change were traditionally known as 'elements', but the word 'transformation' makes the nature of the cycle clearer. Each of these 'transformations' relates to the nine principal numbers that we use in 9 Star Ki astrology.

The Qualities of the Five Transformations

Taking a closer look at these five stages of change will help you appreciate the qualities that they bring to our individual astrological natures. They can be applied to almost any walk of life, activity, food, cooking style, building material, music, artistic expression and so on. In 9 Star Ki astrology, we use the basis of the Five Transformations theory to begin to describe the characteristics of the nine principal numbers. In traditional Chinese medicine these same transformations or elements are used to describe our body organs: fire, for instance, is the driving force behind the heart/small intestine.

Fire

This stage best expresses the full flowering of energy within the cycle. Its nature is upward and outward. In Feng Shui the fire expression is connected with our fame and outward appearance. It represents midday, summer and heat. Individuals with a strong fire presence in their charts tend to be sociable, expressive, warm and passionate.

Soil

This stage represents the result of fire's presence – the creation of ashes, compost and soil. Its nature is more downward and grounding. Soil represents the energy of the afternoon and late summer and is associated with damp or humid weather. Individuals who have soil in their charts tend to be grounded, earthy, practical and, like soil or compost, capable of nurturing and supporting others.

Metal

This stage is a further consolidation of the soil element. Given time and pressure, soil transforms itself into rock and mineral. Its nature is therefore condensing, inward and consolidating. This is the energy of the evening and autumn, a time when we are more at home or begin to gather in the fruits of our labour. The climate associated with this stage is dry. People who have a strong metal presence in their chart tend to be clear and decisive, to pay attention to detail and to have a sense of natural authority.

Water

If minerals and rocks were put under even more intense pressure they would eventually melt. Although we call this stage 'water', it could equally be seen as just fluid. This is the stage in the cycle when energy is floating and appears dormant, just as we are at night and the natural world appears in winter. In terms of climate it represents cold and winter. People who have water in their chart tend to have a quieter, hidden expression that is deep and reflective.

Tree

Water's nature naturally fuels the growth of plants, hence Tree in the cycle. Chinese medicine describes this stage as wood, which is a literal translation and does not really capture the growing/sprouting quality of the Tree. Its nature is associated with the upward movement of energy as well as birth and the beginning of a new cycle. It is associated with the dawn, spring and windy or changeable weather. People with tree energy in their nature tend to have plenty of ideas, energy and enthusiasm, but may lack the ability to complete their tasks.

The Qualities of the Five Transformations

Stage	Nature	9 Star number	Time of day	Season	Weather	Organs	Emotions	Behaviour
Fire	• Upward/outward • Full peak of expression	9	Noon	Summer	Hot	• Heart • Small intestine	+ Warm Passionate – Hysterical	+ Sociable – Erratic Scattered
Soil	• Downward • Grounding	2 5 8	Afternoon	Late summer	Humid Damp	• Spleen • Pancreas • Stomach	+ Discriminating – Cynical Suspicious	+ Grounded Practical – Poor at Finishing
Metal	• Inward • Consolidating	6 7	Evening	Autumn	Dry	• Lungs • Colon	+ Positive Enthusiastic – Depressed	+ Clear Direct – Withdrawn
Water	• Floating • Dormant	1	Night	Winter	Cold	• Kidney • Bladder • Reproductive system	+ Confident – Fearful	+ Adventurous Flexible – Shy
Tree	• Upward • Birth	3 4	Dawn	Spring	Windy Changeable	• Liver • Gall bladder	+ Humorous – Irritable Hypersensitive	+ Fun Spontaneous – Rigid

+ = positive, – = negative

The Interaction of the Five Transformations

The way the five stages interact provides a fascinating insight into our relationships with others. Once you have established whether your principal number is governed by Fire, Soil, Metal, Water or Tree (see pp. 22–4) you can discover how you relate to other individuals. Naturally, if you share a Transformational stage with someone else you will probably have a lot in common. What follows is a description of the two major relationships.

Supporting

In this aspect of the Five Transformations, it is the preceding stage that fuels or supports the next element. For example, fire is the creator of soil, which means that when the fire is fully extinguished it creates soil or ashes in is wake. That soil, when under considerable pressure for a long time, creates the next stage – metal, which in this context means rocks or minerals. Metal, under enormous pressure, will eventually melt and create liquid – which in this context we call water. The water in nature is the natural mother of vegetation such as trees. This wood is the fuel of fire, which completes the 'supporting' nature of this cycle.

Controlling

The nature of this cycle is well understood in traditional Chinese medicine: when a particular organ becomes either hyperactive or sluggish, it has an effect on the element or organ on the opposite side of the cycle. This same theory holds true when we consider our own energetic nature in relation to others around us. We shall look at this closely in Chapter 5, but the principle is as follows:

1. *Fire controls Metal.* Fire can melt metal.
2. *Metal controls Tree.* Metal can cut tree or wood.
3. *Tree controls Soil.* The roots of a plant can break up the soil.
4. *Soil controls Water.* Earth can be used to dam water, or soil can be seen to absorb water.
5. *Water controls Fire.* Water can control fire.

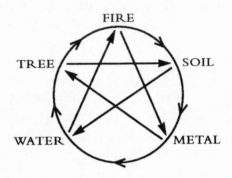

The Five Transformations and 9 Star Astrology

To gain a practical insight into the qualities of these different natural elements, imagine attempting to take a representative of each of these stages in a carrier bag on public transport. It would be relatively simple to carry a plant bought in the market (Tree) or a bag of stones (Metal) or a small bag of compost (Soil). However, a carrier bag full of liquid (Water) would pose quite a challenge, especially if you put it down to pay your fare! You would be in a similar situation trying to transport a flame (Fire). What you can see from these examples is the relative stability of Tree, Soil and Metal's nature compared to the more plasmic qualities of Fire and Water. Although diametrically opposed in nature, they do have similar qualities and these are borne out in 9 Star Ki astrology as they provide both the beginning and the end of the cycle. Water is seen as the most yin element within the spectrum whereas fire is labelled the most yang. Therefore in 9 Star Ki astrology Water is given the number 1 and Fire the number 9.

Soil is traditionally seen as the balancing point or centre of the Five Transformation system, so one of its numbers is 5. Thus soil not only represents the centre of the cycle but is also a buffer between the other elements. As an example, look at what happens between seasons: there is always an indecisive stage when one season finishes and another is imminent. Traditionally, this was known as the Soil stage. Therefore, after Water (1) we have Soil (2), and preceding Fire (9) we have another Soil (8). The rising energy of Tree is given two numbers (3 and 4), as is the contracting nature of Metal (6 and 7).

How to Determine Your Principal Number

In this system all years begin on 4 February and end on 3 February in the following year. So if you were born between 1 January and 3 February remember that your 'year of birth' is the preceding year.

Method 1

For birth years in the twentieth century ignore the first two digits (19) and add up the last two digits. If their sum is less than ten, subtract it from ten to give you the year's number. However, if it is ten or more add these two digits together and subtract their total from ten to give you the year's number. To save the bother of calculating, and to determine the number for people born before and after the twentieth century, see the chart opposite.

Here are some practical examples:

1952
5 + 2 = 7
10 − 7 = 3   **Tree**

1967
6 + 7 = 13
1 + 3 = 4
10 − 4 = 6   **Metal**

1972
7 + 2 = 9
10 − 9 = 1   **Water**

1950
5 + 0 = 5
10 − 5 = 5   **Soil**

1955
5 + 5 = 10
1 + 0 = 1
10 − 1 = 9   **Fire**

9 Star Yearly Numbers 1811–2035

9	8	7	6	5	4	3	2	1
1811	1812	1813	1814	1815	1816	1817	1818	1819
1820	1821	1822	1823	1824	1825	1826	1827	1828
1829	1830	1831	1832	1833	1834	1835	1836	1837
1838	1839	1840	1841	1842	1843	1844	1845	1846
1847	1848	1849	1850	1851	1852	1853	1854	1855
1856	1857	1858	1859	1860	1861	1862	1863	1864
1865	1866	1867	1868	1869	1870	1871	1872	1873
1874	1875	1876	1877	1878	1879	1880	1881	1882
1883	1884	1885	1886	1887	1888	1889	1890	1891
1892	1893	1894	1895	1896	1897	1898	1899	1900
1901	1902	1903	1904	1905	1906	1907	1908	1909
1910	1911	1912	1913	1914	1915	1916	1917	1918
1919	1920	1921	1922	1923	1924	1925	1926	1927
1928	1929	1930	1931	1932	1933	1934	1935	1936
1937	1938	1939	1940	1941	1942	1943	1944	1945
1946	1947	1948	1949	1950	1951	1952	1953	1954
1955	1956	1957	1958	1959	1960	1961	1962	1963
1964	1965	1966	1967	1968	1969	1970	1971	1972
1973	1974	1975	1976	1977	1978	1979	1980	1981
1982	1983	1984	1985	1986	1987	1988	1989	1990
1991	1992	1993	1994	1995	1996	1997	1998	1999
2000	2001	2002	2003	2004	2005	2006	2007	2008
2009	2010	2011	2012	2013	2014	2015	2016	2017
2018	2019	2020	2021	2022	2023	2024	2025	2026
2027	2028	2029	2030	2031	2032	2033	2034	2035

Method 2

This is an alternative method that works for any date in history.

Step 1

Add up all the digits in the year concerned

e.g. 1998, $1 + 9 + 9 + 8 = 27$

Step 2

Add these digits again (if necessary) until they reach a total of 10 or below

e.g. $2 + 7 = 9$

Step 3

Once you have a figure of 10 or below, subtract it from 11

e.g. $11 - 9 = 2$

This now gives you a principal number of 2 Soil for 1998.

3

THE *I* CHING

The *I Ching* (pronounced E King), or *Book of Changes*, is one of the oldest books in the world, and it is from this work that 9 Star astrology, Feng Shui and directionology developed. The *I Ching* was used as an oracle, with folk-sayings handed down through the generations supplying answers to the diviners' questions.

The book is based on eight basic structures called trigrams, which include yin and yang elements (see diagram overleaf). Oriental historians claim that the original trigrams that form this book were formulated by the Emperor Fu Hsi around 3000 BC. The diviner's task was to interpret combinations of these trigrams.

Trigrams and Hexagrams

A trigram is a set of three lines drawn horizontally above each other. Broken lines represent the force of yin and unbroken ones yang. There are eight possible combinations.

A trigram

As you can see from the diagram, the top line represented the influence of heaven, the lower line represented the influence of earth, and sandwiched between these two forces was humanity. The interpretation of these trigrams was intended to guide humanity as it navigated its way through life influenced by the forces of heaven and earth. The *I Ching* uses two trigrams placed one on top of the other to form a hexagram, which offers more profound answers to the diviner's questions.

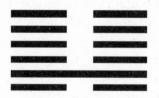

Hexagram No 7 from the *I Ching*

When the eight trigrams are turned into hexagrams in this way, 64 combinations are possible. Traditionally, to determine which hexagram they should consult people would either use stalks of the yarrow plant or toss three coins on six occasions. The coin method is the simpler of the two. Throw the three coins and then count three for heads and two for tails. If the total of the three coins makes an odd number, draw an unbroken line. If they make an even number, draw a line with a gap in the centre. Repeat this six times to form a hexagram from the bottom to the top. The interpretation of these hexagrams has been refined over the centuries; the most recent and best-known work was that done by Confucius around 500 BC.

The *I Ching* is an excellent source of guidance and intuition. If you own a copy, look after it and do not allow other people access to it. In this way only your own Ki energy pervades the book, allowing for more accurate and insightful interpretations of your questions. For consulting the *I Ching* I use coins, all of the same denomination and all kept very clean and only used for this purpose. When formulating a question, I keep the coins in my hands. The questions need to be short, simple and unambiguous.

The *I Ching* and 9 Star Astrology

In Feng Shui the trigram can be used to represent a particular area of your plot of land or home, or an individual room. In 9 Star Ki astrology the eight trigrams represent the eight traditional members of the family: father, mother, eldest son, eldest daughter, middle son, middle daughter, youngest son and youngest daughter. However, gender is irrelevant – the 'father', for instance, can be male or female, as explained below. The information from the trigrams, together with the transformational stage described in Chapter 2, helps to build the character of the nine stars.

The core of this system, as in the Five Transformation system and in Feng Shui, is what is called the Tai Chi. This is the centre around which the other transformational stages or rooms or family members pivot. The unique nature of this central space will be covered in Chapter 7, and as you read through the family qualities of the eight trigrams you will find that 5 Soil, being the centre, has no trigrams.

This central quality of 5 Soil is similar to that of Saturn in Western astrology. It represents the beginning and the end of the cycle. Similarly Mars represents Fire, Mercury Water, Jupiter the Tree element and Venus the Metal element.

Father (Heaven) 6 Metal

The three yang lines here represent the full male quality. The 6 Metal person, whether male or female, will come across as a very straightforward individual with a natural air of authority. In families, schools, communities and the workplace they are noted for their quiet, fair way of dealing with situations. However, in their quest for fairness they can sometimes appear too rigid.

Famous examples past and present include Dr Christiaan Barnard, Napoleon Bonaparte, Vivien Leigh, Robert Mugabe, Bruce Springsteen and the Duke of Wellington.

Mother (Earth) 2 Soil

With its three broken yin lines this trigram has all the yin feminine qualities. These include receptiveness, helpfulness, supportiveness, diplomacy and caring. Whether male or female, the 2 Soil individual tries to provide a fair and open chance for everybody.

Famous examples past and present include Benazir Bhutto, Mahatma Gandhi, King Hussein of Jordan, J.F. Kennedy, the Dalai Lama and Abraham Lincoln.

Eldest Son (Thunder) 3 Tree

The yang line at the bottom gives some stability to the yin growing phase represented by the two broken lines. As the first-born, the Eldest Son is able to try things out for the first time, to discover and explore, to make mistakes and be a little impetuous in his actions. Whether male or female, the Eldest Son is scouting the route for his future siblings.

Famous examples past and present include André Agassi, Diana, Princess of Wales, Michelangelo, Elvis Presley, Margaret Thatcher and Vincent Van Gogh.

Eldest Daughter (Wind) 4 Tree

Here the yin line is at the bottom with the two yang lines above, symbolising a somewhat slower growth than that of the Eldest Son. However, like the Eldest Son, the Eldest Daughter is always searching for new approaches in her expression and work. Her somewhat impetuous behaviour can lead to mistakes.

Famous examples past and present include Janis Joplin, Lawrence of Arabia, Lenin, Paul McCartney and Yoko Ono.

Middle Son (Water) 1 Water

Sitting in the middle of the family, the Middle Son is able to help resolve conflicts. The softer, quieter and reflective qualities of water soften what would otherwise be a heated argument or debate.

Famous examples past and present include Louis Armstrong, Queen Elizabeth the Queen Mother, Billy Graham, Nelson Mandela, Helmut Schmidt and Queen Victoria.

Middle Daughter (Fire) 9 Fire

Where her same-level brother might listen and subsequently come up with a diplomatic win/win situation for everyone, the 9 Fire will come to conclusions very quickly. The fire that she brings to the party is that of shedding light on the problem in hand. She comes to the point quickly and helps those around see what is obvious. Her challenging and direct nature can dazzle as well.

Famous examples past and present include Winston Churchill, Bill Clinton, Freddie Mercury, Mussolini, Eva Peron and Mother Teresa.

Youngest Son (Mountain) 8 Soil

This member of the family has the benefit of the accumulated experience of everybody else's trials and tribulations. He therefore has more opportunity for reflection. The Youngest Son is very good at expressing this accumulation of experiences through a more intellectual approach.

Famous examples past and present include Charles Dickens, Germaine Greer, Salman Rushdie, Mao Tse-tung, Voltaire and Tennessee Williams.

Youngest Daughter (Lake) 7 Metal

Like her brother (8 Soil), the Youngest Daughter brings the wealth of experience that coming into the family last can provide. As with her brother, it is the reflective quality that comes through, presented in a more emotional, spiritual and amusing way.

Famous examples past and present include Helena Bonham-Carter, John Cleese, D.H. Lawrence, Rembrandt, Tina Turner and Boris Yeltsin.

Seventh Child (the Centre) 5 Soil

There is no trigram to represent the 5 Soil individual as he has qualities drawn from all eight trigrams. The unique quality of these people is that they relate well to, and draw from, all other members of the family. They are often at the centre of the family and situations. Some commentators on the *I Ching* and 9 Star astrology claim that the 5 Soil person brings the quality of 2 Soil and 8 Soil to their character. The 5 Soil often acts independently from the rest of his family. He can break new ground easily, take the heat where others would wilt, and is not afraid to be involved in new projects or new ideas.

Famous examples past and present include Muhammad Ali, Richard Branson, Stephen Hawking, Elizabeth Taylor, the Duchess of Windsor and the Duchess of York.

4

THE NINE PRINCIPAL
NUMBERS

This chapter introduces the nine principal numbers that
form the basis of your astrological chart associated with
9 Star Ki astrology. To calculate your own or someone
else's yearly number, see pp. 22–4 and the chart on
p. 23.   This gives you a starting point for understanding your fundamental nature, which will be dealt with in
Chapters 7 and 8.

The information below on each of the nine principal
numbers has been divided for convenience and easy reference as follows:

- *Years*
  A list of years that share the same principal number in
  nine-year cycles.

- *Trigram*
  The trigram, drawn from the *I Ching*, that represents
  the year in question.

- *Symbolism*
  Each trigram has a unique symbolism drawn from
  translations of the *I Ching*. All are essentially examples
  of natural forces or elements.

- *Interpretation*
  My interpretations of the traditional symbolism of the trigrams, adapted to astrology rather than to Feng Shui.

- *Family member*
  Each trigram represents a family member (see Chapter 3) and gives you another way of understanding your principal number by interpreting the nature of your position within the 'family'.

- *Element*
  Drawn from the Five Transformations theory (Fire/Water/Soil/Tree/Metal).

- *Colour*
  A representation of the element from the Five Transformations theory, drawn primarily from the element in the natural world.

- *Character*
  The basic qualities of each star.

- *Health*
  Drawn from traditional Chinese medicine, this section explains what can support and what can damage the organs controlled by your 'element'.

- *Occupations*
  A list of occupations best suited to the nature of each of the nine principal numbers.

- *Personal development*
  How to get the most from your principal nature.

- *Examples*
  A list of individuals past and present who share principal numbers. This helps you to see a pattern and acts as a reference for reflecting on the character (see earlier in this list).

Number 1 White Water Star

Years

1864, 1873, 1882, 1891, 1900, 1909, 1918, 1927, 1936, 1945, 1954, 1963, 1972, 1981, 1990, 1999, 2008, 2017, 2026, 2035

Trigram

K'An

Symbolism

Water – The North

Interpretation

The trigram is composed of one yang line encapsulated by two yin lines which seem to be symbolically trapping the yang or the depth within them. This can be interpreted as a sign of hidden strength, symbolic of nature's dormancy during winter. While all seems quiet and lifeless, major change is taking place beneath the surface of the earth. The *I Ching* interpretation of the trigram is that there is hidden strength and depth behind a facade.

Family member

Middle Son

Element

Water

Colour

White or transparent

Character

To appreciate fully the qualities of the Number 1 White Water Star, we must look at the qualities of water in nature: on the one hand the lively, fresh mountain stream epitomised by waterfalls and activity, and on the other the deep, slow, calm qualities of ponds, lakes and oceans. Many 1 Water characters fall into one or other of these categories. The spirited, youthful nature of a fresh mountain stream brings out a spirit of adventure. One of water's qualities is its natural exploratory tendency, always looking for the next opportunity to move on in search of the sea. This argument is borne out by the number of famous explorers born under this sign. Water also needs some kind of container, from a glass to the banks of a river. Without this containment its free-spirited nature can result in individuals being chaotic and undisciplined. The opposite quality also holds true: from time to time, the Number 1 Water type can seem too disciplined and too rigid – for example, the Ayatollah Khomeini.

The sensitive, philosophical and intuitive side of water's nature is exhibited in the many artists, writers and composers born under this sign. This brooding, reflective quality is similar to the energy of deep water.

The trigram K'An, which represents the Middle Son, brings out the diplomatic quality in some White Water stars. You could be a good arbitrator or lawyer as well as being a good listener within the family and community. Although you may seem quiet on the surface you hear all sides of the argument and will often come up with a win/win situation. Two contemporary examples are Nelson Mandela and F.W. de Clerk, who worked out a win/win situation for the peoples of South Africa. Such people are the deepest thinkers within the 9 Star Ki astrology system, and are perhaps the most intense and spiritual. They generally find listening easy, and written communication comes naturally to them.

Number 1 Water individuals value their own space and prefer to be independent. As a result they can become isolated and may spend much of their middle and old age alone. Queen Victoria and her husband Prince Albert shared the 1 Water star; when Albert died, Victoria withdrew into herself for the rest of her long life. This behaviour can be taken to extremes and in some cases appears paranoid. A recent example of such behaviour in a 1 Water individual was ex-President Ceaucescu of Romania, who governed by caution and fear and withdrew from the world so greatly that he became a recluse. He ended up rigid and tyrannical, which led to his downfall in 1989.

The element water, which in oriental medicine governs the functions of the kidneys, bladder and reproductive system, is always associated with sexual energy. Libido and sexual attraction are qualities that generally feature strongly within the 1 Water person. They exhibit great passion but are not flirtatious by nature, and once they make a commitment it is generally very deep.

Health

The main concern for the 1 Water person is to take care of the systems controlled by water – kidneys, bladder, reproductive system and adrenals. Traditionally, keeping warm and well-rested nurtured the quality of the element water that supported these systems. The best advice is to get plenty of sleep, to keep warm, and to avoid too much alcohol, coffee and sugar and too many late nights. It is also sensible to avoid living in damp and cold environments. Generally those people do not have the most robust of health and need to take care of their circulation too.

Occupations

The deep, reflective qualities of 1 Water make these individuals excellent authors, poets, composers, philosophers,

musicians or therapists. Their innate quality for finding balance in argument provides a sound basis for being a lawyer.
The adventurous nature of water has created many famous
explorers. When 1 Waters can express their deep nature
they make excellent entertainers. Finally, any field of work
that involves the management, creation or distribution of
'liquids' fits with the 1 Water nature. This could involve
working with fuels, alcohol, inks, dyes and anything that
need the support of water, such as fish, shellfish and algae.

Personal development

The strong, independent nature of 1 Waters coupled with
their potential difficulty in communicating what is happen-
ing inside them can lead to isolation. Make the effort to
socialise more and allow others access to your remarkable
intuition and sense of humour.

- Design a regular routine of physical activity to pro-
  mote your circulation

Examples

Apart from those already mentioned:

Politicians and rulers
Fidel Castro, Catherine the Great, Anwar Sadat

Explorers
Captain Cook, Sir Francis Drake, John Blashford-Snell

The arts
Ingmar Bergman, Enrico Caruso, Frédéric Chopin, Eric
Clapton, Errol Flynn, James Joyce, Diane Keaton, Percy
Bysshe Shelley, Alexander Solzhenitsyn, Igor Stravinsky,
Andy Warhol

Sports personalities
Chris Evert, Peter Schmeichel, Rory Underwood

Number 2 Black Soil Star

Years

1872, 1881, 1890, 1899, 1908, 1917, 1926, 1935, 1944, 1953, 1962, 1971, 1980, 1989, 1998, 2007, 2015, 2024, 2034

Trigram

K'Un

Symbolism

Earth – The Receptive

Interpretation

The trigram is made up of all three yin lines, representing the full force of earth and the maternal qualities that she brings. Far from being a weak trigram, it indicates a strong consistent nature with the desire to serve, while at the same time needing the support of yang which can be provided by any one of the other trigrams.

Family member

Mother

Element

Soil

Colour

Black

Character

The maternal quality that this trigram reveals best serves 2 Soil individuals when they are in a position of service to others. They are not natural born leaders, but work away in the background and quietly get the job done. For steadiness and reliability the Number 2 Soil is unbeatable.

The quality of soil represented here could be described as sand or compost, which gives us the image of its nurturing, helpful nature. The earthly and maternal nature that the 2 Soil possesses is expressed not only within the individual's family but within the larger family of humanity. There are many examples in history and in the present of leaders whose main aim was or is to serve others.

Number 2 Soil individuals are not aggressive by nature and have a strong, patient quality. They are generally sociable and public-spirited and make excellent teachers or organisers. Busying themselves by helping others gives them great satisfaction. They need to be within a group, whether family, workplace or elsewhere: without the support of an organisation they can lose direction and spirit. These types tend to be over-fastidious and fussy in their working methods, which can cause them to get bogged down in detail and irritates others. On the plus side, as representative of 'mother' and 'birth' they derive great strength from using their natural talent for diplomacy. King Hussein of Jordan is a fine example of the Number 2 Soil 'diplomat', frequently reported in the media as endeavouring to create solutions in the Middle East that are acceptable to both Arab countries and Israel.

The Number 2 Soil person often feels at home on the land or in the woods. Gardening or walking in the country are good forms of recreation.

Health

The Number 2 Soil has a sensitive quality and does not have a very tough constitution. In traditional Chinese medicine, the element soil controls the function of the spleen, pancreas and stomach; these three central organs are also held to be responsible for the lymphatic and immune system. Number 2 Soil people should take care of the pancreas in particular, as it is the linchpin of the soil-controlled system. This means they must restrict refined carbohydrates, ice cream, dairy products, sugar, sweets and chocolate. Since the number 2 type is controlled by the element soil, it is equally their strength. Here are some suggestions:

- Chew very well
- Eat small amounts, and eat fairly often (to keep the blood-sugar level consistent)
- Include plenty of grains and grain-based products in your diet
- Introduce foods such as malts and fruits that provide natural sugar

Since 2 Soil types are more yin than yang they should take care of their immune system. This means allowing your body to adapt to changes in climate, so:

- Avoid too much central heating and air conditioning and too many long, hot baths

Occupations

Positions of service – to humanity, to your country, to local politics or whatever – work well for 2 Soil people. Other areas where help and service are essential include nursing, and the 2 Soil's skills of listening, diplomacy and tact would be most useful in a career as a social worker. Service-related occupations such as shopkeeper, bank clerk, shop assistant or personal assistant, are also suitable. As the 2 type is controlled by soil, any career in agriculture or horticulture is appropriate.

Personal development

Make time and space for yourself: 2 Soils have enormous capacity for helping others, but at the same time they need to re-create their own energy. Find a balance between work and play, giving and receiving, leading and being led. Some may gain strength from being on the land, perhaps by growing vegetables in the back garden or by taking long walks in the country.

- Take plenty of fresh air and exercise to avoid physical stagnation

Examples

Apart from those already mentioned:

Politicians and rulers
Tony Blair, Ho Chi Minh, Michael Portillo

Explorers
Roald Amundsen, Hernando Cortes

The arts
Michael Douglas, Thomas Gainsborough, Marilyn Monroe, Luciano Pavarotti, Pablo Picasso, Diana Ross, Oscar Wilde

Inventors
Sir Alexander Fleming, Samuel Morse

Religion and philosophy
The Dalai Lama, Nostradamus

Number 3 Bright Green Tree

Years

1871, 1880, 1889, 1898, 1907, 1916, 1925, 1934, 1943, 1952, 1961, 1970, 1979, 1988, 1997, 2006, 2015, 2024, 2033

Trigram

Chen

Symbolism

Thunder – the Awakening

Interpretation

This trigram has at its base a strong yang line opening up into the two yin lines which represent growth and action. The symbolism is that of the awakening qualities of spring and the dawn, which translate into strong movement and action grounded in the strength of yang. This representation of the three lines could manifest as spontaneity and action, with more emphasis on 'doing' than 'being'.

Family member

Eldest Son

Element

Tree

Colour

Bright green

Character

These individuals are born with the full force of spring within their nature. Like the season, they are endowed with plenty of vitality and energy and are capable of strong, powerful action. They are very positive and optimistic, going about their tasks vigorously and expecting others to keep up. In their pursuit of growth or new pastures they may lead the way and leave the details to others.

The symbolism of thunder has an explosive and awesome quality. As in nature, thunder indicates that some change is about to occur. People who dislike change and interruption in their lives dislike the vigorous and optimistic nature of the 3 Tree. They are open and honest, and can be unerringly frank to the point where they alienate friends and colleagues. They like to get their point of view across first, and only then will they listen to the thoughts and opinions of others. These strongly opinionated people can have grandiose ideas, but if they can complement this by working with others who can 'ground' their vision they can be one of the most creative of the 9 Star types.

As the Eldest Son of the 9 Star family, 3 Trees are likely to be precocious. Many born under this sign have early success in their lives and move on as soon as they become bored. The full energy of spring that the sign represents also gives 3 Trees a strong, virile nature, and many figures in the entertainment world who have this sign are regarded as pin-ups or heart-throbs.

Many people born under this sign are humorous and outspoken and frequently get themselves into trouble through their direct and honest sense of humour. Fortunately their articulacy can just as easily get them out of such situations! Spontaneity, humour and charm are amongst the strongest assets of a 3 Tree.

Health

The element tree, associated with the Number 3 personality, governs the function of the liver and gall bladder in traditional Chinese medicine. To strength these two organs:

- Avoid eating for two to three hours before going to sleep
- Avoid over-eating
- Reduce saturated animal fats in your diet
- Avoid late-night drinking, eating and entertaining (1-3 a.m.), as this is the time when the liver is recharging itself
- Introduce plenty of green leafy vegetables into your diet
- Eat lightly fermented pickles and good-quality vinegars, which help the liver and gall bladder
- Skip a meal once or twice a week
- Make an effort to be up early in the morning as the dawn (like spring) is associated with the function of the liver and gall bladder
- Take some kind of physical exercise in the morning before eating to help stimulate the liver and release stored energy in the form of glycogen

Occupations

The Number 3 Tree has enormous potential for planning and defining what needs to be done. These people can see the path ahead while others may get bogged down in details. They can pick their way through a minefield of difficulties and provide vision and inspiration to move forward. Their physically strong and flexible nature makes them potentially excellent sportsmen and women, also energetic performers and speakers. Breaking new ground in the arts and sciences is also one of their strengths.

Personal development

Probably the best advice for the spontaneous and ground-breaking Number 3 Tree is to make time to reflect and to complete projects. In social and work situations, they should make the effort to listen more to those around them. They should remember that their positive and vital nature can be daunting to some as well as an inspiration to others.

- Balance your great bursts of energy by building up your reserves: sleep, holidays and rejuvenating body-work such as aromatherapy massage can all help

Examples

Apart from those already mentioned:

Politicians and rulers
Adolf Hitler, Cecil Rhodes, Lech Walesa

The arts
Brigitte Bardot, Samuel Taylor Coleridge, Claude Debussy, Mick Jagger, Henry Moore, Robert de Niro, Laurence Olivier, Marcel Proust, Keith Richards, Robin Williams

Inventors
It is interesting that the Thunder trigram which represents the 3 Tree is seen as a powerful elemental force. All these men harnessed powerful forms of energy: Ernest Rutherford, James Watt, Sir Frank Whittle

Religion and philosophy
Friedrich Nietzsche

Sports personalities
Frank Bruno, Jimmy Connors, Billy-Jean King, Alan Shearer

Number 4 Green Tree Star

Years

1861, 1870, 1879, 1888, 1897, 1906, 1915, 1924, 1933, 1942, 1951, 1960, 1969, 1978, 1987, 1996, 2005, 2014, 2023, 2032

Trigram

Sun

Symbolism

Wind

Interpretation

The top two yang lines of this trigram represent steadiness and consistency. Unlike the 3 Tree, the 4 Tree has a stable quality. The lowest line, which is yin, indicates a gentle nature that needs support from its roots. While overall the trigram shows stability, it is the underlying receptive quality of the first line which gives way to this softer nature beneath.

Family member

Eldest Daughter

Element

Tree

Colour

Green

Character

The Number 4 Tree has a nature that, from a Western astrological point of view, is governed by 'air'. The trigram wind can denote anything from stillness to a full-fledged hurricane, and as a result the Number 4 Tree is one of the most emotional of the nine signs. While at times appearing gentle and easy-going, these individuals can change their moods quickly and can become stubborn and impulsive.

Although they share the tree-like nature of number 3, they are a lot more practical, thoughtful and reliable. They have great common sense and sensitivity to others. This can work both for and against. Sensitivity, when combined with good listening skills, can make for an excellent counsellor, but on the other hand it can make these people easily influenced by more powerful individuals. This trusting quality, innate to 4 Trees, can make them gullible.

Their sensitivity makes them deeply appreciative of poetry, painting, music and other arts. Their best form of communication is conversation, and they can be very charismatic orators, leaders or political figures. The natural element of wind can cause them to change their minds frequently, also their direction in life. On the other hand, the gentle quality of wind can allow their influence to pervade their work, their direction and their relationships.

The trusting nature of 4 Stars can cause difficulties in relationships as they regard everyone as trustworthy. It is a good idea to seek the advice of a friend or confidant before embarking on a long-term commitment in a relationship. The facial expression of 4 Stars, in particular the eyes, appears very open; this is a sign of trust rather than intrusiveness.

Health

Like the Number 3 Tree, the Number 4 needs to protect and strengthen the liver and gall bladder. The more yang liver is more closely associated with 3, and the gall bladder with 4. Here is some advice:

- Do not eat too quickly
- Do not eat when you are distracted (talking, standing, walking, reading, watching television, arguing)
- Do not eat cold dairy products
- Do not drink ice-cold fluids
- Do not eat when you are not hungry

The gall bladder rules our sensitivity to the environment, and its effect is seen in our response to:

- Smells
- Noises
- Bright sunlight
- Touch or sensations on the skin

Meditation and relaxation techniques are beneficial for the Number 4 Tree, as they help to offset the tendency to be in constant 'planning mode'.

Occupations

A positive use of the Number 4 Tree's attributes lies in the field of planning and mapping out future projects, whether you organise travel itineraries (travel agent) or work out how to get a load from A to B (transport). These individuals' adaptable and harmonious nature can also be put to good use in public relations, broadcasting and film-making. A famous example of someone who used his Number 4 Tree nature in the field of communications was Baron von Reuter, founder of the news agency.

Personal development

It is wise to try to become less sensitive to the influence of the behaviour and ideas of others, and to develop self-assertiveness. Because of your open nature you can upset others by talking too freely about other people's private lives, even though you do so without malice. Seek advice from a third party regarding relationships and financial planning.

- To help protect yourself from being easily swayed by influences in your life, develop a regular practice of meditation such as T'ai Chi Chuan, Chi Kung or yoga, that helps to 'centre' you

Examples

Apart from those already mentioned:

Politicians and rulers
Charles I, General Gaddafi, Stalin

The arts
Kenneth Branagh, Joan Collins, Jimi Hendrix, Raphael, Martin Scorsese, William Shakespeare, Orson Welles

Inventors
John Logie Baird, Galileo

Religion and philosophy
Martin Luther, Rudolf Steiner

Sports personalities
Damon Hill, Ayrton Senna

<u>Number 5 Yellow Soil Star</u>

Years

1851, 1860, 1869, 1878, 1887, 1896, 1905, 1914, 1923, 1932, 1941, 1950, 1959, 1968, 1977, 1986, 1995, 2004, 2013, 2022, 2031

Trigram

None

Symbolism

The centre

Interpretation

Nine Star Ki astrology is based on the *I Ching*, which has eight trigrams. The Number 5 Soil represents the axis on which those eight revolve and therefore has no trigram of its own, but draws its nature from the others. In some interpretations of 9 Star Ki astrology, Number 5 Soil is seen as a combination of the 2 Soil and the 8 Soil nature.

Family member

Although 5 Soil is essentially part of the family, his life and activities are relatively distant from those of the other members. In *The Nine Ki Handbook*, Steve Gagné and John Mann describe the 5 Soil as the Seventh Child. This infers that he brings a very different quality to the family, an outside influence, even a more poetic or spiritual dimension.

Element

Soil

Colour

Yellow

Character

Being at the centre of this system of astrology, as a 5 Soil you will always find yourself at the centre of what is going on. At work you will frequently be at the hub of discussions or arguments and will probably feel left out if this is not the case. In family life you will let your opinions and needs be known to those around you. You have a great capacity to control situations and are likely to take the lead.

People often look to you for leadership and guidance. While at times this can be fulfilling and exhilarating, friends could lean on you and take advantage. If you are off your guard or not feeling well you could find this a drain. At these times you need to protect yourself from being exploited in this way.

The 5 Soil House in 9 Star astrology is symbolic of the beginning and end of a cycle. In relation to your principal nature this could be defined as a life of ups and downs, which in some situations could be quite extreme, involving success or failure. However, you should not take this negatively as 5 Soil people have great resilience and bounce back in times of difficulty. It is not unusual for 5 Soil individuals to make similar mistakes throughout their lives, but their resilient natures help them deal with challenges far more quickly than any of the other eight characters.

Your ideas and style may appear unorthodox, and you need to guard against being over-ambitious or too impractical. You tend to take criticism or advice as a threat, which can make you either defensive or even more determined. You are bold and determined, sometimes aggressively so, and can bring about enormous change through reinvention or the destruction of old systems or patterns. Being outside the 'family', symbolic of the so-called Seventh Child, gives you a tendency to learn in life from outside the family – from your own difficulties and experiences. As a result it is not unusual for you to develop and stabilise later in life.

Perhaps the best image of the 5 Soil nature is a toddler. If you watch children of two or three explore and experience the world it can be fascinating and frustrating at the same time. They wander around the home like a miniature sumo wrestler, wide-eyed, determined, inquisitive, with a tremendous strength in their belly as they totter from one activity to the next. Yet there is no weakness in their gait – all toddlers are very resilient and centred. They cannot be held back as they explore, make mistakes and bounce back from some new discovery that turned out to be painful or frightening. They look as if they own the world.

In relationships, since you are at the centre people will naturally gravitate towards you – and you enjoy having that attention focused on you. As a result you may find yourself in unusual circumstances – for instance, being involved with someone much older or much younger. There may be further complications in the relationship due to divorce, step-children and so on. Similarly, you may find yourself in some kind of love triangle.

Health

Potentially you have the constitution of an ox, which gives you the greatest capacity to bounce back from stress-related problems and general health problems. However, for the same reason you must remember to exercise and challenge yourself. As with any complex machine, unless you use it to its full potential it is likely to seize up through inactivity.

- Avoid being lazy about exercise, and make the effort to stimulate your circulation vigorously at least three times a week

The ups and downs in your nature can make you go to extremes, which means going through phases of being active/inactive or slim/overweight. Many of these negative traits are likely to be brought on by the emotional events in your life at the time.

In Chinese medicine Soil is the controlling factor for the function of the spleen, the pancreas and the stomach. In terms of Ki energy, these organs are disrupted by excessive worry and anxiety. You therefore need to make more effort than others to cope with and share your worries as swiftly as possible, rather than slip into lethargy and depression.

Occupations

Being at the centre, you have the best possible chance of bringing people together, for instance in diplomacy or politics. Many, such as Richard Branson, have become successful entrepreneurs. For some 5 Soils, their unorthodox, ambitious and dominant nature has made them famous or flamboyant military leaders. Being in any position of control or authority is a comfortable setting for the Number 5 Soil. But their earthy nature finds many of them in quite mundane occupations. Some make a great success of wheeling-and-dealing as second-hand car salesmen or market traders or in door-to-door sales. Others put their social talent to good use by running pubs, restaurants and clubs.

Personal development

You will always find yourself drawn into the centre of whatever is going on. This can be stimulating but, when you feel vulnerable, it can be draining.

- Pace yourself well and avoid getting burnt out
- Try to find some time every day to be with yourself and reflect on where you are and where you are going

- Find some activity or pursuit to keep you centred: T'ai Chi Chuan, Chi Kung, meditation, yoga or a martial art

Examples

Apart from those already mentioned:

Politicians and leaders
David Ben-Gurion, Jacques Chirac, Oliver Cromwell, Mahatma Gandhi, General Gordon, Chiang Kai-shek

Explorers
Thor Heyerdahl, Sir Walter Raleigh

The arts
Richard Attenborough, Ludwig van Beethoven, Lord Byron, Anton Chekhov, Greta Garbo, Henri Matisse

Religion and philosophy
John Calvin, Jean-Paul Sartre

Sports personalities
Joe Dimaggio, Michael Schumacher

6 White Metal Star

Years

1850, 1859, 1868, 1877, 1886, 1895, 1904, 1913, 1922, 1931, 1940, 1949, 1958, 1967, 1975, 1985, 1994, 2003, 2012, 2021, 2030

Trigram

Ch'ien

Symbolism

Heaven

Interpretation

The three yang lines are an indication of the full force of heaven, bringing consistency, strength and boldness of character. There is no 'if', 'but' or 'maybe' with this character. But this powerful yang combination can lack balance – yin would have to be supplied by the sensitive, imaginative and appreciative nature of those around them.

Family member

Father

Element

Metal

Colour

White

Character

The most obvious trait is that of natural leadership and authority. This can be in the field of politics and militarism or fashion and the arts. Many 6 Metals have broken new ground and paved the way for future generations. Examples include the inventors Sir Clive Sinclair, the breaker of the monopoly of international airlines Sir Freddie Laker, the surgical transplant pioneer Dr Christiaan Barnard, the Regency arbiter of taste and fashion Beau Brummell, and the eighteenth-century landscape gardener Capability

Brown. With the full force of heaven present in your tri-gram, as a 6 Metal you can be extremely moral, direct and noble. The consistent nature of the three lines can make you rational, careful, sometimes even rigid. You are active and sociable, but more reserved than the Number 7 Metal. You tend to be a perfectionist and are quietly self-critical. The worst mistake that anyone can make with a 6 Metal friend is to criticise them.

Most 6 Metal types place a lot of emphasis on family values. You are natural leaders in the family and the community, and will often give up your outside interests to return to the home if that is what the situation warrants. If you do not have a family of your own you may well be at the hub of activity in the workplace. You are a born leader in most situations. Many captains of international sports have been 6 Metals.

In relationships you are the most loyal of all the nine types and are at your most comfortable in a relationship where you can take the lead. Despite the fact that you are governed by the full force of yang the opposite side to this nature can come through, showing up as a strongly intuitive individual with a rational, wise approach to family and relationship problems.

Health

You need to protect the lungs, the yang organ that is controlled by the Metal element, so guard against any activity that can weaken what is really your constitutional strength.

- Avoid smoking
- Take plenty of aerobic exercise
- Make sure that you 'get things off your chest': express any pent up emotion to prevent its negative qualities stagnating in your lungs
- Include plenty of green leafy vegetables in your diet

In traditional Chinese medicine, the lungs also control the function of the skin, which is regarded as the third lung. People of this sign are prone to asthma, eczema, rashes, depression and chronic digestive problems. The autumn is a powerful time for you to reflect and make changes in your diet and way of life.

Occupations

You are a natural leader and would make an excellent job of such a role in business, politics, the armed forces and many other fields. Your great sense of justice can make you an excellent lawyer. As a 6 White Metal person you enjoy heat, pressure and stress far more than do any of the other signs, and are wise to engage in careers that challenge you.

Personal development

Good advice for you would be to work on bringing out your warmer and gentler nature.

- Find time to relax and unwind
- Spoil yourself: take yourself shopping or luxuriate with a relaxing aromatherapy massage

Always consider other people's requirements as well as your own, in particular what other people actually want rather than what you think they may need. Your natural capacity for leadership and seeing situations clearly can make you come across as overbearing.

- Try to develop your listening skills on all levels

Your strong active qualities can be developed further in team sports.

- Rather than playing one-to-one sports such as bad-minton and tennis, try to be one of a team

Examples

Apart from those already mentioned:

Politicians and rulers
Mikhail Gorbachev, Richard Nixon, Yitzhak Rabin

Explorers
Captain Scott, Amerigo Vespucci

The arts
Sir Arthur Conan Doyle, Salvador Dali, James Dean, Marlene Dietrich, Placido Domingo, John Le Carré, John Lennon, Auguste Renoir, Sharon Stone, William Wordsworth

Inventors
Johannes Kepler, J. Robert Oppenheimer

Religion and philosophy
Thomas Hobbes, Desmond Tutu

Sports personalities
Geoffrey Boycott, Paul Gascoigne, Jesse Owens, Daley Thompson

<u>Number 7 Red Metal Star</u>

Years

1867, 1876, 1885, 1894, 1903, 1912, 1921, 1930, 1939, 1948, 1957, 1966, 1975, 1984, 1993, 2002, 2011, 2020, 2029

Trigram

Tui

Symbolism

Lake

Interpretation

This trigram has a solid base of two yang lines which open up to the softer, reflective nature that manifests as water on the surface – hence the imagery of the Lake. Number 7 Metal individuals conceal a deep, inner security beneath a visible outgoing, fun-loving spirit. Other interpretations of the *I Ching* call this trigram Joy.

Family member

Youngest Daughter

Element

Metal

Colour

Red

Character

The time of year associated with the 7 Metal is late autumn, when farmers traditionally celebrated the harvest with relaxation and enjoyment. Number 7 Metal types are great pleasure-seekers who, more than any other of the nine stars, enjoy spending money on fashion, entertainment and eating out. At the table you make a great host, with a capacity to listen and be receptive to others. You often dress and appear younger than your natural age.

Like the 6 Metal you have leadership qualities, but these are displayed in the advice you give others or the direction you suggest in the workplace. You are charismatic, flamboyant and graceful in nature. You have a great sense of fun and optimism and are endowed with a good sense of humour. With your free and independent nature you are not keen to be drawn into long-term commitments at work or in relationships. Being the Youngest Daughter, you have the accumulated experience of the rest of the family to help you.

Your articulacy and sense of timing make you an exceptionally good speaker, and many 7 Metal politicians were famous orators. Number 7 Metal individuals often exhibit a swing in character between their outgoing, fun-loving, sociable side and a deeper, reflective, spiritual nature.

Health

The element metal controls the function of the colon or large intestine. To look after your colon:

- Do not over-eat
- Avoid late-night eating
- Chew slowly
- Reduce your intake of baked flour products such as cakes, pies and biscuits
- Reduce your intake of saturated animal fats (eggs, cheese, meat), especially when heavily cooked (pâté, roast meats, smoked fish)

All traditional cultures have some form of fermented food in their diet which strengthens the colon. Products of this kind that are readily available include natural live yoghurt, soups flavoured with soy sauce or miso, pickles, vinegar, wine, light traditional ales and fermented fish such as pickled herrings.

Occupations

Since the element metal controls your sign, you would do well handling money and would make a very good financial advisor, stock controller or accountant. Your speaking skills would be useful to you as a teacher, lecturer or counsellor, or in local or national politics. Your sociable, fun-loving nature would make you a good manager of fashionable restaurants and clubs. Your leadership and accounting qualities, together with your interest in food, would help you in the food processing, packaging and distribution industries as well as in quality control of food.

Personal development

- Try to develop your generosity, financially and emotionally
- Try to take on tasks that test your perseverance, and make every effort to see them through to their completion

Your easy-going nature may lead you to forget the importance of physical activity. Since metal controls the lungs/colon:

- Make the effort to do vigorous exercise such as jogging or cycling at least three times per week

Examples

Apart from those already mentioned:

Politicians and rulers

Benjamin Disraeli, Helmut Kohl, William Pitt the Younger, the Prince of Wales, William Wilberforce

Explorers

David Livingstone

The arts

Peter Bogdanovich, Robert Burns, Sean Connery, Francis Ford Coppola, D.H. Lawrence, Andrew Lloyd Webber, Claude Monet, Harold Pinter, Michelle Pfeiffer, Peter Tchaikovsky, Richard Wagner

Inventors

Sir Isaac Newton, Louis Pasteur

Sports personalities

Eric Cantona, Sally Gunnell, Mike Tyson

Number 8 White Soil Star

Years

1857, 1866, 1875, 1884, 1893, 1902, 1911, 1920, 1929, 1938, 1947, 1956, 1965, 1974, 1983, 1992, 2001, 2010, 2019, 2028

Trigram

Ken

Symbolism

Mountain

Interpretation

Yang in the top or 'surface' line conceals inner strength and contemplation. The imagery of the mountain is that of a strong, immovable exterior with a cooler, more withdrawn interior. This trigram is associated with the transition from winter to spring – a quiet, reflective period paving the way to new growth. Some interpretations of the *I Ching* call this trigram Contemplation.

Family member

Youngest Son

Element

Soil

Colour

White

Character

As the Youngest Son, the Number 8 White Soil has the combined experience of the older brothers and sisters. You have a good natural sense of investment and frequently accumulate wealth when young, through either your own hard labour or an inheritance. If your investment or business fails before middle age, you are quite likely to succeed again. Your success in achieving material wealth tends to be achieved more through your single-mindedness than through any subtlety, charm or creative talent: Alan Bond and Ronnie Biggs are two examples.

The most yang of the three soil types, you tend to move slowly and persistently and to gain from your experiences.

The mountain imagery shows you to be a strong, stable character with enormous reserves of energy – although you need to retreat into your 'cave' from time to time, which gives the impression of being reserved and cool in most situations. Of all the nine signs you are perhaps the hardest to get close to: you generally conceal your feelings and only display them when provoked. When you are challenged, you can dart out of your 'cave' and deliver a powerful argument.

You have a strong sense of what is right and just, and many 8 Soils have been involved in human rights. The mountain, combining qualities of strength and contemplation, can bring about change and revolution in people's lives. But you can be resistant to change not initiated by you. Your main asset is your composed, solid nature that can ride out most difficulties in life. Your experience and hidden strength can be of enormous help to family, friends and colleagues.

Health

Number 8 Soil types tend to be hypochondriacs. This is partly due to their contemplative, reflective nature, which can make them too concerned with aches, pains and symptoms. Their strength of constitution needs to be challenged by strong physical exercise and they should guard against becoming overweight, lethargic or self-indulgent. The involvement of soil means that if you are this type you need to pay particular attention to the function of the pancreas:

- Avoid all forms of refined sugar and refined carbohydrate in general
- Avoid strong stimulants such as coffee, chocolate and spices which cause the blood sugar level to fluctuate

Traditional oriental advice for imbalances of the pancreas includes the following:

- Rub the skin vigorously, especially the hands and feet, with a hot, damp towel in the morning and evening
- Eat naturally sweet foods such as fruit, sweet vegetables and malt from grains

Occupations

The pragmatic, loyal nature of the Number 8 Soil type lends itself to service-related activities: jobs such as shopkeeper, accountant, hairdresser or delivery agent. Where other star types may have the ideas or the qualities of leadership, you have the greatest capacity to produce and deliver: you would not, for instance, be a newspaper editor, but you would be a very good sub-editor, production assistant or researcher. Your innate feeling for argument and justice makes you a capable police officer, lawyer, trade union official or human rights activist.

Personal development

Try not to let your strong sense of justice and fairness turn into self-righteousness. Engage your powerful capacity for argument and reflection in a creative way. This could mean getting involved in local or national debates and political issues.

- Focus on keeping your body flexible and adaptable: yoga is ideal. However, as an 8 Soil you have a tendency to stagnate your energy, so make sure you practise a dynamic style of yoga such as Oki or Iyengar yoga

Examples

Apart from those already mentioned:

Politicians and rulers

Yasser Arafat, Queen Elizabeth I, Hermann Goering, Ronald Reagan

The arts

José Carreras, Paul Cézanne, Edward Elgar, Paul Gauguin, Elton John, Grace Kelly, Beatrix Potter, the Marquis de Sade, Stephen Spielberg

Religion and philosophy

Pope John Paul II, Martin Luther King, Albert Schweitzer

Sports personalities

Will Carling, Martina Navratilova, O.J. Simpson

Number 9 Purple Fire Star

Years

1856, 1865, 1874, 1883, 1892, 1901, 1910, 1919, 1928, 1937, 1946, 1955, 1964, 1973, 1982, 1991, 2000, 2009, 2018, 2027

Trigram

Li

Symbolism

Fire

Interpretation

The two yang lines encapsulating a softer yin line can be interpreted as an individual with an energised exterior. Strength, vanity and brilliance hide a softer nature which can manifest as a lack of confidence, a self-critical, doubting quality which makes you seek acknowledgement and support from those around you.

Family member

Middle Daughter

Element

Fire

Colour

Purple

Character

The Number 9 Fire person has all the qualities that the sun can bestow – inspiration, enlightenment and clarity. These types have an enormous capacity to see the obvious and steer a path through troubled waters. In politics, particularly in times of change and revolution, they can inspire a nation. Their natural active energy attracts them to situations that are in a similar state of flux, or, conversely, their natural strong charge attracts them to situations of stagnation that require major change. Mother Teresa and Florence Nightingale are two examples of this category.

Of all the nine stars this is the one most at home in the field of communication – especially when it concerns emotions and personal experiences. These traits, along with your warm, passionate nature, can make you successful in theatre and film. The enlightened liberal views of 9 Fires are well represented by the poet and artist William Blake, but 9 Fires can equally be proud, vain, sophisticated and critical.

The sensitive nature that underlies your strong, successful surface image can erupt stormily, but of all nine types you are the quickest to forgive and forget. Like your brother the Middle Son (1 White Water) you do not like to have your space invaded, and as a result have few close friends but plenty of contacts. Your capacity to see clearly and understand the big picture does not help you deal with the practical problems of day-to-day living such as repairing the washing machine or changing the oil in your car!

Appearances are important to you. In clothes, cars and the contents of your home you pay considerable attention to detail and dislike individuals who seem sloppy or untidy or who display poor manners.

The world would be a poorer place without the colourful, sophisticated, inspiring Number 9. You lift the spirit and inspire us with your performance, and you are certainly not going to be forgotten overnight.

Health

In traditional Chinese medicine fire controls the function of the heart and small intestine. The hyperactive 9 Fire type needs to guard against possible circulatory disorders and good advice would be:

- Avoid smoking
- Avoid too much salt and soy sauce
- Avoid saturated animals fat in foods such as eggs, cheese, butter, meat and smoked fish
- Take up some form of deep reflective relaxation that incorporates your need for some activity: the moving, flowing meditative quality of T'ai Chi Chuan is ideal

Your sensitive, active nature is also largely driven by your nervous system, so:

- Do not over-stimulate or over-sensitise your nervous system with recreational drugs or too much coffee, sugar or spicy food

Occupations

You are well suited to any job where contact with the public is involved. The more you can express yourself, the happier and more powerful you will be. Careers in politics, music, singing or acting are all appropriate. Advertising and marketing are also excellent, particularly if you own the company. Your natural flair for communications would give you a good career in customer service, television, radio or photography.

Personal development

Your Fire nature can easily highlight that which is obvious – especially for others; this and your deep-seated intuition are your great strengths. However, a good fire needs to be grounded by a firm basis in the fuel and the hearth.

- Try to develop your practical nature in all aspects of your life

Examples

Apart from those already mentioned:

Politicians and rulers

General Franco, Che Guevara, Saddam Hussein, Jomo Kenyatta, Marshal Tito

Explorers

Christopher Columbus, Francisco Pizarro

The arts

Jane Austen, Johann Sebastian Bach, Warren Beatty, Walt Disney, David Hockney, Franz Kafka, Stanley Kubrick, Liza Minnelli, Sylvester Stallone, J.R.R. Tolkien, W.B. Yeats

Inventors

Alexander Graham Bell, Enrico Fermi, Bill Gates

Religion and philosophy

William Booth, Guru Nanak, Jean-Jacques Rousseau, John
Wesley

Sports personalities

George Best, Monica Seles, Greg Norman, Ilie Nastase

5

RELATIONSHIPS

From Chapter 4 you will have been able to determine your own principal number. At this stage it is also worth determining the principal numbers of other people in your life – family, friends, colleagues and so on – so that you get a feeling for the principal nature of as many Houses as possible. This information will enable you to make broader and more objective judgements of the people around you, not solely based on your understanding of your own number.

The next step is to examine how your principal nature would interact with the other eight numbers. Begin to observe how your fundamental nature can potentially best support, or be supported by, other numbers using this system. This is just a starting point, however, and as you develop deeper insights into your other two numbers in Chapters 7 and 8 you will see that the potential for using this system can be infinite.

There are two basic ways to look at relationships in terms of 9 Star Ki astrology. First there are the relationships within the 'family of the *I Ching*', and then we can take a closer look at the Five Transformation theory in terms of 9 Star Ki astrology.

The *I Ching* Family

Chapter 3 explained the symbolism of the nine Houses relative to the trigram from the *I Ching* that each represented. Essentially the nine numbers stood for the Mother, the Father, the three Daughters, the three Sons and the so-called Seventh Child. Looking at your principal number in this way, try to formulate the relationship that your own member of the family would have in terms of the other members. What follows are my insights and views – feel free to make your own interpretations as well.

Father (6 Metal)

This number always brings a strong, active and authoritative quality to bear on all members of the family. There may be a special relationship with the Eldest Son (3 Tree) and the Mother (2 Soil), and there is always a special place in every Father's heart for the Youngest Daughter (7 Metal).

Mother (2 Soil)

Her nature is to support and help all members of the family. Naturally there will be a special relationship with the Father (6 Metal) and potentially some discord with the Daughters (4 Tree, 9 Fire and 7 Metal)!

Eldest Son (3 Tree)

This is the ground-breaker, the pioneer of the family, perhaps with a special relationship to the Father (6 Metal).

Eldest Daughter (4 Tree)

The first-born daughter takes on many responsibilities from the Mother (2 Soil), and can be supportive of her or rebellious. She can be an inspiration or guidance to her younger sisters (7 Metal and 9 Fire).

Middle Son (1 Water)

Always looking for a win/win situation in family life and arguments, the Middle Son is helpful, diplomatic and potentially very much at ease with all the members of the family.

Middle Daughter (9 Fire)

Bright, bubbly and enthusiastic, the Middle Daughter can be engaging and illuminating in conversation and in action. Like her brother the Middle Son (1 Water), she can bring the potential of diplomacy to family conflict.

Youngest Son (8 Soil)

Potentially, he can get support from his older brothers (3 Tree and 1 Water). He has a special relationship with the Mother (2 Soil). Like his sister the Youngest Daughter (7 Metal), he may appear to take things easy and remain unaffected by turbulence.

Youngest Daughter (7 Metal)

She can appear easy-going and laid-back, as the rest of the family have made the mistakes and had the early struggles. At the same time there is a special relationship with the Father (6 Metal) and possibly also the Mother (2 Soil).

Seventh Child (5 Soil)

Always at the centre, the Seventh Child has the greatest potential to relate well to the other eight members of the

family. The 5 Soil's nature can be controlling and demanding but essentially at the centre of family life; alternatively, it
can be someone who is outside the family.

The Five Transformations

A far more scientific way of looking at relationships, this
theory is used as the basis for diagnosis in traditional Chinese
medicine in which the various transformational stages relate
to different organs of the body. The theory is also used in
Feng Shui for determining balancing features in the home
or workplace: the various stages can relate to different den-
sities of material, colour, lighting, environmental factors and
so on.

You can employ any of the following three methods, as
appropriate.

Same transformation

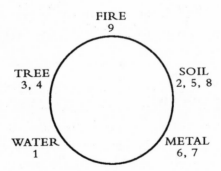

Use this method where you share a transformational num-
ber with somebody else – for instance you are both 3
Tree, or one of you is 3 Tree and the other 4 Tree.
Basically you share a Tree nature. The interpretation here

is that of a relationship in which your energy is similar, which we could call the brother/sister relationship. You have a profound understanding of each other through having the same nature and family, which can lead to a quiet, mellow, gentle relationship with little spark or antagonism. Perhaps this is the kind of relationship that you want – or perhaps not. We all know people who thrive on antagonism and the unexpected in their life – this combination, which can lead to lifelong partnerships and friendships, is not for them.

Supporting relationship

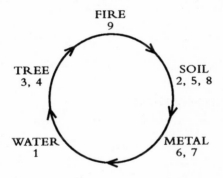

This is where one element supports the next. The cycle shown in the diagram infers that Soil supports Metal, Metal supports Water, Water supports Tree and so on. This is known as the mother/child relationship. It may appear that the traffic is purely one-way, but it can reverse as well: in the diagram 80 per cent of the energy is moving clockwise and 20 per cent flowing back in the opposite direction. Again, this is potentially a stable relationship whether at work or within the family.

Antagonistic relationship

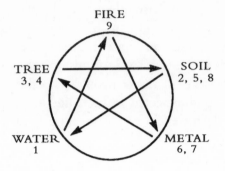

This form of relationship can easily be misunderstood – just the word 'antagonism' suggests negativity. What you can see here is that when one of the transformational stages becomes hyperactive it tends to ignore the stage that it could be supporting to cut across the cycle and potentially block or give spark to the opposite stage. For example, Water has the potential to dampen Fire, Fire can potentially melt Metal and so forth. Some of the most exciting and passionate relationships can be found in this combination. In work situations you could feel your creativity and talent being thwarted by this combination. Another interpretation is that your potential, rather than being undermined, could be encouraged by this antagonism. It does not necessarily have to be viewed negatively.

Here are some well-known historical and contemporary examples of relationships, using these three fundamental principles.

Brother/sister relationships

Fire and Fire

The rock star David Bowie (9 Fire) and his wife the model Iman (9 Fire).

Soil and Soil

Hollywood stars Micky Rourke (8 Soil) and Carrie Otis (5 Soil). The professional collaboration of humorous librettist William Gilbert (2 Soil) and composer Arthur Sullivan (5 Soil).

Metal and Metal

Two men of the same age who were at Oxford together and became lifelong friends, William Wilberforce and William Pitt the Younger (both 7 Metal). French Impressionist painters Edouard Manet (6 Metal), Auguste Renoir (6 Metal) and Claude Monet (7 Metal).

Water and Water

Queen Victoria and Prince Albert (both 1 Water) were inseparable in life, and after Albert's early death from typhoid in 1861 his widow withdrew from public life for many years.

Tree and Tree

The Hollywood screen combination of Jack Lemmon and Tony Curtis (both 3 Tree), the political combination of Lenin and Trotsky (both 4 Tree), the inseparable relationship of Lauren Bacall and Humphrey Bogart (both 3 Tree), and the actress Ingrid Bergman and her one-time husband director Roberto Rossellini (both 4 Tree).

Mother/child relationships

Water supports Tree

Probably one of Hollywood's most famous relationships was that of Spencer Tracy (1 Water) and Katharine Hepburn (3 Tree). Roger Vadim (1 Water) met Brigitte Bardot (3 Tree) in the 1950s, made her a star and married her. Goldie Hawn (1 Water) and Kurt Russell (4 Tree) have been together for many years and have three children.

Tree supports Fire

The artist and painter El Greco (9 Fire) studied in Rome and was influenced by the work of Michelangelo (3 Tree). Adolf Hitler (3 Tree) and his support for Benito Mussolini (9 Fire).

Fire supports Soil

There are many famous examples of working combinations of these two elements. They include jazz musicians Django Reinhardt (9 Fire) and Stéphane Grappelli (2 Soil), and the brilliant minds of Peter Cooke (9 Fire) and Dudley Moore (2 Soil). The duo who first conquered Mount Everest in 1953 were Edmund Hillary (9 Fire) and Sherpa Tenzing (2 Soil); both men have always claimed that they reached the summit together and have refused to say which of them led the final assault. The British ballerina Dame Margot Fonteyn (9 Fire) created one of the most memorable part-nerships in the history of ballet with Rudolf Nureyev (8 Soil). Friedrich Engels (9 Fire), the German philosopher and co-founder of Marxism, supported the Marx family and completed *Das Kapital* after the death of Karl Marx (2 Soil).

Soil supports Metal

Wallis Simpson (5 Soil) and King Edward VIII (7 Metal), later known as the Duke of Windsor; in his abdication speech in 1936 Edward said, 'I have found it impossible to carry the heavy burden of responsibility and to discharge my duties as King as I would wish to do without the help of the woman I love.' The Middle East peace process negotiated by Yitzhak Rabin (6 Metal) would not have been possible without the support of Yasser Arafat (8 Soil). The composer Richard Rodgers (8 Soil) first worked with the librettist Lorenz Hart (6 Metal), and after Hart's death began the famous collaboration with Oscar Hammerstein II (also 6 Metal) which produced *Oklahoma, South Pacific, The King and I* and *The Sound of Music*.

Metal supports Water

Nell Gwyn (7 Metal) and King Charles II (1 Water); despite having many other mistresses Charles remained devoted to her and on his deathbed pleaded 'Let not poor Nelly starve.' After the death of Prince Albert, as described above, Queen Victoria (1 Water) withdrew into herself; the greatest support she received was from her Prime Minister Benjamin Disraeli (7 Metal) and her son the future King Edward VII (6 Metal), who as Prince of Wales carried out many of her duties.

Antagonistic relationships

As can be seen from the diagram, elements/transformations of an opposite nature can give 'over-riding' or 'controlling' qualities to each other.

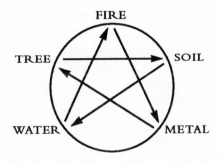

This use of the so-called 'control cycle' is a direct legacy from oriental medicine. It is not always an antagonistic situation – it is only so when one of the elements becomes hyperactive. In other words, the antagonistic quality will only come to the surface when the antagonist/controller is in a more powerful position emotionally or energetically. For example, in Chinese medicine the element of water controls the function of the kidneys, and it is well known that in acute kidney failure there is often a corresponding effect on the heart (fire). Similarly, people with acute heart failure experience breathing difficulties as the lungs are controlled by the element metal.

The basic argument is:

- Fire melts Metal
- Metal cuts Tree/wood
- Tree (and its roots) breaks up Earth
- Earth absorbs Water
- Water controls Fire

Fire melts Metal

Winston Churchill (9 Fire) and Hitler's deputy Rudolf Hess (7 Metal), who flew to Scotland during World War II to negotiate a peace settlement and found himself imprisoned instead. In Hollywood the combination of Bruce Willis (9 Fire) and Demi Moore (6 Metal).

Metal cuts Tree

After the death of Russia's notorious dictator Joseph Stalin (4 Tree) in 1956 he was publicly denounced by the next Russian Premier, Nikita Khrushchev (7 Metal). Brooke Shields (7 Metal) and André Agassi (3 Tree).

Tree breaks Earth

Henry VII (3 Tree) succeeded to the English throne in 1485, having killed Richard III (8 Soil) at the Battle of Bosworth. General George Custer (8 Soil) was killed in 1886 at the Battle of Little Big Horn by Sioux warriors led by Sitting Bull (4 Tree). The artists Vincent Van Gogh (3 Tree) and Paul Gauguin (8 Soil), although friends, also quarrelled badly; it was after one such quarrel that Van Gogh famously cut off one of his own ears.

Earth absorbs Water

These are two examples of relationships which broke down in a blaze of publicity: Woody Allen (2 Soil) and Mia

Farrow (1 Water), Martina Navratilova (8 Soil) and her lover Judy Nelson (1 Water).

Water controls Fire

From his exile in the West, Ayatollah Khomeini (1 Water) helped to orchestrate the revolution that overthrew the Shah of Iran (9 Fire) in January 1979.

Looking for Personal Patterns

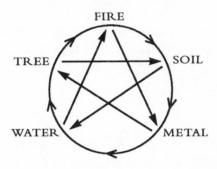

At this point it would be useful to draw a large circle as above, place the Five Transformations in position, draw in the appropriate arrows for the supporting and controlling sides of the cycle, and put yourself on the map. Now begin to add names against the different elements of people in your life, and see if you find a pattern. Any so-called 'antagonism' can equally be used to help you relate better to the individual or individuals concerned through having a new perspective on the relationship.

6

THE MAGIC SQUARE

To take the system of 9 Star Ki astrology further, we now need to study what is called the Magic Square and its various permutations in order to discover two more layers in our astrological chart.

Origins

According to Chinese tradition, the Magic Square was discovered in the markings that appeared on the shell of a tortoise as it emerged from the River Lo some four thousand years ago. The numbers presented themselves in a series of dots within nine sections of the creature's shell (see below).

This was translated into the grid that appears below, and over the centuries has been known variously as the Magic Square, the Lo Map or the Lo Shu Square. The reason for the description 'magic' is that whichever way you add up the numbers they total 15. For example, $4 + 5 + 6 = 15$, $4 + 9 + 2 = 15$, $9 + 5 + 1 = 15$ and so on.

The sequence of squares is also associated with the eight basic trigrams of the *I Ching* discussed in Chapter 3. Remember that the central square had no trigram because the other squares rotated around it.

Uses

Directionology

One of the primary uses of the Magic Square is in directionology. The space occupied by 9 at the top of the Magic Square is facing the 'Fire' – in other words the sun and therefore the south. Opposite this, facing the north and the cold and the winter, is the square 1. In the east, representing spring and the dawn, is number 3; followed by a continuation along this theme, occupying the south-easterly position is number 4. The gathering forces of the evening or the autumn are represented in the west by number 7 and in the north-west by number 6. The soil/earth qualities of 2, 5 and 8 are represented in the centre (5), in the south-west (2) and in the north-east (8).

	SOUTH	
4	9	2
3	5	7
8	1	6

S E / S W / EAST / WEST / N E / N W / NORTH

Feng Shui

In some intuitive forms of Feng Shui the Magic Square is known as the Bagua or Pa-Kua. The spaces in the Bagua grid represent different functions of space within our home or workplace. This grid is laid over either the entire plot or the whole house or each room. The gateway, entrance, door or whatever is regarded as being on the lower line (that is, 8, 1 or 6).

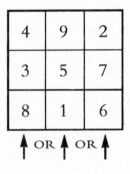

Number 1 space represents our direction in life, our career. Number 2 space represents our relationships, our marriage and our cooperation with others. Number 3 space represents our parents, our teachers and our ancestors. Number 4 space represents our prosperity, our luck and general wealth. Number 5 (which has no trigram) represents our health and is the centre of the system and of our home or room. The recommendation is always to keep this space clutter-free. Number 6 space represents outside help – support from beyond our space and our own support for others. Number 7 represents our children and our projects. Number 8 space (remember the symbolism here was Mountain) is the space for contemplation, study, reflection and stillness. Number 9 space (represented by the trigram for Fire) is about our recognition in the world – this could be what we are best known for, and it is also represented as an 'inner flame', inspiration.

Relationship with the *I Ching*

The diagram above combines the relationships of the Magic Square and the trigrams of the *I Ching*, and it will be a useful reference tool later on in Chapters 11, 12 and 13. With time and practice you can add your own commentary to these interpretations, as so many have done over the past four thousand years.

Number 1

Trigram: Kan
North
Water
Water/transparent
Dormancy,
   winter,
   retreat,
   inaction

Number 2

Trigram: Kun
South-west
Soil
Black
Hidden potential,
   germination,
   fertility

Number 3

Trigram: Chen
East
Tree
Bright green
Early spring,
    new ideas,
    vitality,
    impulsiveness

Number 4

Trigram: Sun
South-east
Tree
Green
The maturation of spring,
    the full expression of
    upward growth, wealth
    and prosperity

Number 5

No trigram: the
    centre of the Bagua
Central
Soil
Yellow
Symbolic of growth,
    the transition from seed
    to harvest

Number 6

Trigram: Chien
North-west
Metal
White
Clarification,
    responsibility,
    accomplishment

Number 7

Trigram: Tui
West
Metal
Red
Harvest, maturation,
    self-reflection, insights

Number 8

Trigram: Ken
North-east
Soil
White
Change,
    revolution,
    turning point,
    new direction

Number 9

Trigram: Li
South
Fire
Purple
Brightness,
    summer, midday,
    realisation, illumination

The Importance of the Central Number

So far we have looked at the nine spaces within the Magic Square and some examples of what each represents. However, there are eight further variations around this Magic Square. From the pattern overleaf you can see that as this happens the central number changes progressively backwards (9, 8, 7, 6, 5 and so on). These nine squares will enable you to discover your second and third numbers to complete your birth chart, and to predict 'where' you are in Chapters 11 and 12. They also form the basis of the directionology that is discussed in Chapter 13.

8	4	6
7	**9**	2
3	5	1

7	3	5
6	**8**	1
2	4	9

6	2	4
5	**7**	9
1	3	8

5	1	3
4	**6**	8
9	2	7

4	9	2
3	**5**	7
8	1	6

3	8	1
2	**4**	6
7	9	5

2	7	9
1	**3**	5
6	8	4

1	6	8
9	**2**	4
5	7	3

9	5	7
8	**1**	3
4	6	2

7

YOUR CHARACTER NUMBER

You will have discovered from Chapter 4 the qualities of the star that was present in the year of your birth (your natal star) which reveals your basic nature and energy. This so-called principal or constitutional number is particularly relevant when you begin to see where you are in any given year and month (Chapters 11 and 12). The second or central number – your character number – reveals two important qualities about you – your character and who you were as a child, or who you revert to being under pressure.

Character

Our basic character, personality and emotions are far more present in this central number than in the other two numbers. What comes through strongly is the driving force behind who you are. When we express ourselves in a relationship, or under pressure, what we reveal to others is this central number. It is our deep spiritual quality as well as our spontaneous nature that comes into force when called upon. For example, a person may have a constitutional first number that has a quiet, insightful and serious side, such as 1 Water, but the second, central number may reveal that the underlying characteristic is Fire or Tree, which responds very differently from Water.

Childhood

This central number is also regarded as the constitutional quality that we have until we have completed two nine-year cycles (18 years) or until we gain independence and leave home, which is generally around the age of 18. Basically, we are this second number until we reach adulthood. This becomes interesting to study when we look at who we were as children relative to our siblings, parents and teachers, which will be covered at the end of this chapter. It also makes understanding our own children fascinating.

Under pressure, it is not uncommon to revert to our childhood nature. In such situations our response can be quite different from that associated with the constitutional number that we work with daily. For example, if our character number is 8 Soil (Mountain) we may, if pushed, argue powerfully or retreat into our 'cave'. We may, as children, have wanted to spend more time alone or studying, or to be more distant from our family, and may well have been misunderstood.

How to Discover Your Character Number

From the chart below, find your principal number in one of the three column headings on the right. Now look up your day and month of birth in the left-hand column, and then look across to tie this up with the number in the particular right-hand column under the heading where you found your principal number.

For example, if your date of birth is 13 November 1954 it gives you a principal number of 1 Water. The number 1 appears in the first of the right-hand column headings (along with 4 and 7). Looking down the left-hand column, you will find 13 November in the period 8 November to 7 December. Looking across to the corresponding line in the first right-hand column, you will see that the appropriate character number is 8. Taking your first and central numbers together, this gives you a reading so far of 1.8. This chapter, however, concentrates on the character number, the '8' in the example.

Birth Date	1, 4, 7	5, 2, 8	3, 6, 9
4 February to 5 March	8	2	5
6 March to 5 April	7	1	4
6 April to 5 May	6	9	3
6 May to 5 June	5	8	2
6 June to 7 July	4	7	1
8 July to 7 August	3	6	9
8 August to 7 September	2	5	8
8 September to 8 October	1	4	7
9 October to 7 November	9	3	6
8 November to 7 December	8	2	5
8 December to 5 January	7	1	4
6 January to 3 February	6	9	3

The Number 1 character

These individuals tend to keep their emotions and thoughts to themselves and often appear shy and aloof. The hidden, deep nature of water often expresses itself in a more reserved and nonchalant fashion. When these people do make decisions, therefore, they often surprise those around them by the apparent suddenness of their plans. Sometimes their natural fluidity leads them to go with the flow in stressful situations. Under pressure they may make a decision which goes against a more cautious approach, and at a later date they may regret having done so. When fully expressed, the depth of Water's passionate nature can surface in vivaciousness, charm, flamboyance and magnetism (Boy George, Prince, Elton John, Donald Trump).

Although they often appear sociable in public, this may well be a cover for their more reserved nature. The 1 Water character is also deeply intuitive and compassionate, which can lead these people to involvement in charitable work.

Examples

Lauren Bacall, Diana, Princess of Wales, Bob Geldof, Che Guevara, Stephen Spielberg, Sting. It is interesting that the first five drivers in the 1995 Formula One world championships all had central numbers of 1: Michael Schumacher, Damon Hill, David Coulthard, Johnny Herbert, Jean Alesi.

The Number 1 child

What these children especially need is encouragement to socialise, expand their horizons and explore, whether by travel or reading. An over-protective stance on the parents' part makes matters worse.

The Number 2 character

The trigram is that of Earth – Mother, the feminine expression. These individuals are generally reliable, devoted, helpful and dedicated to their work and families. They have a natural flair for being tactful and frequently sacrifice their own needs for the sake of others. They genuinely want to help and be involved, whether with their family or at work with colleagues, and can therefore be exploited. The 2 central number is often the first person to say, 'I can take that home and get it done by Monday morning.'

However, they often lack the self-confidence of other central numbers. If they receive overt criticism or if acknowledgement is not forthcoming this can feed their insecurity, causing them to lose confidence and become withdrawn, depressed and tired. Serving others fulfils their compassionate nature and helps to strengthen their confidence. Many Number 2 Soils get caught up in detail to the point of obsession and need others to remind them of the main issue. They are old-fashioned and reserved in their behaviour and outlook on life. Given that the Number 2 Soil is essentially a female expression, men who have this central number may make more show of their masculine gender.

Examples

Yasser Arafat, Naomi Campbell, Charles Dickens, John McEnroe, Oliver Reed, Debra Winger.

The Number 2 child

Given that the trigram for 2 Soil is three (broken) yin lines, the best support for this child is consistency from parents and teachers. Number 2 children need a routine and kept promises. They have a strong diplomatic nature and may find themselves brokering peace between squabbling siblings or in neighbourhood arguments. This is the first child to let you know if he or she has been unfairly dealt with.

What can damage their character are parents who do not keep their word and who set certain moral standards but do not observe them themselves. Living in a high-rise city flat, with little access to nature and few outings to the country or holidays may damage the fundamental quality of Soil for this child.

The Number 3 character

In the natural world, the quality behind this character is that of the full force of spring or the awakening of dawn. These people are progressive in their thinking and action, they are always visibly active and enjoy initiating and discussing new ideas and projects. Whether it is at work brainstorming a new design or suggesting social arrangements for a Saturday evening you can guarantee that their ideas, expression and energy will be present. However, their enthusiasm wanes when the conversation comes down to details. Sometimes they can take on too many activities at once, which gives the impression of a chaotic character.

Being the Eldest Son in the *I Ching*, they have an adventurous, impulsive nature. Their mood (Thunder) can affect everyone around them. If they are happy, bright and fulfilled, others will feel the same. If, however, they are angry and frustrated it will rub off on those near them. None of us enjoys defeat, whether physical or emotional, but the vanity of the Number 3 character takes it very personally. Not having their own way can lead to frustration and then anger – but, like thunder, it will soon roll on!

Examples

Marie-Antoinette, Saddam Hussein, Martina Navratilova, Jack Nicholson, Al Pacino, Oscar Wilde.

The Number 3 child

The best support is to allow the 3 Tree child to explore his or her ideas and creative talents to the full. If they show an interest in ballet, car maintenance, surfing or whatever, encourage them to keep up their interest and do any practice necessary. They are naturally curious, so try not to dampen their curiosity by ignoring their questions.

These children like to socialise and are the last to come in from the playground. Being the Eldest Son, they are often precocious and take an earlier interest than the other signs in parties and meeting the opposite sex. Their physical appearance and clothing are important to them, and they find criticism of these deeply offensive. The most damaging thing for them is for their nature to be suppressed in any way.

The Number 4 character

Of all the nine characters in this system of astrology, the 4 Tree is perhaps the most adaptable. The relevant trigram, Wind, has a yin bottom line with two strong yang lines above, which symbolises a strong outward nature that does, however, need support. Taking this with the symbolism of Wind, you could interpret the 4 Tree as a changeable and adaptable nature. Sometimes, like the wind, these people can seem scatty and chaotic; at other times they may appear moody.

They also have a strong emotional nature which is expressed in a very open way. It is not like the Thunder of the 3 Tree character, but more affectionate and loving. They enjoy being appreciated, while at the same time they can get satisfaction from helping others.

They can be influenced by their immediate surroundings. Whether this is the health, wellbeing or emotional state of their partner, or the pressure they are under at work, either way it will have a deep effect on them. Some characters in this system can easily cope with stress, but not so with the 4 Tree type.

They have a very open and trusting nature, a quality which can work in two different ways. First, they can bring influence to bear on others by generating enormous trust for what they say and do. This can make them extremely influential in their communication – especially verbal. The second aspect is their almost unquestioning trust in others which verges on gullibility. They believe that everyone is potentially trustworthy, and perhaps should get a second opinion from a close friend or confidant before embarking on a new relationship or a new partnership based on trust.

Four Tree characters are persistent people who are not afraid of getting on with the job themselves and, conversely, do not delegate easily. They need to be wary that no one exploits them.

Examples

Marianne Faithfull, Mahatma Gandhi, Steffi Graf, John Major, Lord Mountbatten, Sharon Stone.

The Number 4 child

These children have tremendous potential for creativity and breaking new ground, so they need plenty of encouragement from parents and teachers. It is especially important to show appreciation for their efforts and to give them constant inspiration. They need plenty of space and time to display their creative potential.

What can damage these children is to suppress their creativity and dreams in any way. If they show early signs of talent in a particular field encourage it and do not dismiss it. But because of their 'changeable' nature (Wind) they need to be made aware of their commitments and to be cautious about trusting everyone around them.

The Number 5 character

The outward expression of this character seems bold and demanding to the point of aggressiveness. This is because of the innate leadership potential of the 5 Soil character. Driven by their own needs, they can be very assertive when it comes to making demands. Like a diamond, they can be very strong, self-protective and extremely persevering.

Being at the centre of this system of astrology they can have a controlling influence on whatever they are involved in, at work or at home. The 5 Soil character can exhibit extremes: some are incredibly creative or ambitious, while others are unenthusiastic and lazy or have no goals in life. However, whatever route they take they have the strength to overcome difficulties. They also learn more readily from their mistakes and have the capacity to bounce back more quickly than any of the other signs. They have a great talent for self-preservation.

They hold themselves in high esteem and do not happily take advice or criticism from others. They do, however, have a genuine concern for those around them, and it is not uncommon for people to be drawn to them for help or advice.

Examples

Boris Becker, Richard Burton, Winston Churchill, Joan Collins, Clint Eastwood.

The Number 5 child

These children need a stable family and school life, with parents and teachers as a reference point. Being at the centre of this form of astrology, it is hard for them to navigate a clear path. Without appropriate guidance they develop in their own way and are very open to the influences of others – for better or worse.

It is damaging to the 5 Soil child if others take advantage of his or her supportive nature. If this happens, as adults they may become withdrawn, suspicious and reserved.

The Number 6 character

These people have a very direct, down-to-earth, uncompromising nature. This is primarily influenced by the trigram Heaven, which forms the basis of their character. They frequently stand for what is logical, just and ethical, and as a result can be opinionated and inflexible.

They have a very clear opinion of what is right and what is wrong. Combine this with their confident nature and you have a character who can communicate in a very direct way. These characters have the greatest potential for leadership, and others often find themselves charmed or organised by these people.

They tend to be perfectionists and are highly critical of their own standards and work. As a result, they do not take criticism well. They have enormous pride and it hurts them deeply to lose face.

There can be a quieter, introverted, almost intuitive quality about them also. This can appear as shyness, but in reality Number 6 characters tend to play their cards close to their chests. They do not necessarily broadcast their plans to the world for fear of the criticism or lack of confidence that other people may voice.

Having a full yang quality in their make-up, they need a good source of yin; this could be someone who could provide them with advice. It is important for them to have the opportunity to express their ideas privately and get feedback in a non-intimidating way. This prevents them from becoming too isolated, too rigid or too domineering in their pursuits.

Examples

Rowan Atkinson, Shirley Bassey, Richard Branson, Kevin Costner, Ernest Hemingway, Jackie Onassis.

The Number 6 child

The best support for this child is moral guidance and confidence. They have a natural ability to pick up on what is right and need parents and teachers to show them flexibility and debate. It is important for them not to become opinionated or isolated because of their ethical standpoint.

The biggest potential damage is caused by criticism. These children are hypersensitive, proud and strongly self-critical anyway. Be wary not to harm their enormous confidence at a young age by suppressing or demeaning them in any way.

The Number 7 character

These individuals seem easy-going and adaptable. The imagery of their character is the Lake, which appears calm on the surface, hiding emotions, dreams and schemes deep within. Many express themselves diplomatically, others romantically or nostalgically.

They are usually very expressive and entertaining, with a great sense of humour. They can be extremely witty, and of all the nine characters are the most persuasive when speaking in public. Some can appear nervous in their expressions; however, this is not a true reflection of their deeper yang nature.

One of their great strengths is their capacity to listen to, endorse and encourage others and to make them feel the centre of their attention. This is an excellent quality for a host. Number 7 characters have patience and the skill of helping people feel comfortable in any situation.

Their trigram – Joy or the Lake, and its representation within the family of the *I Ching* as the Youngest Daughter – is confirmation of their fun-loving, entertaining, witty nature. The other side of their nature can be deeply private: they have the potential to draw not only on their own life experiences but also on the wisdom of their predecessors, especially in the field in which they are engaged.

Examples

Marlon Brando, Mel Brooks, Michael Caine, Barbara Castle, Susan Sarandon, Peter Sellers.

The Number 7 child

The best support for these children is to give them a social lifestyle. They have a naturally fun-loving nature that is best cultivated by plenty of social interaction at home and at school. They have a naturally independent spirit which can be encouraged by allowing them wider boundaries.

Probably the most damaging influence on the development of a 7 Metal child is to be over-indulged or spoilt. This could make them demanding, extravagant and over-bearing as they reach adulthood. Being lonely and isolated in their formative years can make this naturally gregarious character introverted and timid in later life.

The Number 8 character

Of all the nine personalities this is the most private. Number 8 characters value their own space and are verbally uncommunicative, but may find other channels for self-expression such as music, work and art.

The Mountain symbol that accompanies their trigram gives them a hard shell with a soft underbelly. This gives people the impression that they are calm and stable, and friends will turn to them for counsel. The symbolism of the Youngest Son can give Number 8 characters an impulsive and energetic nature, keen to be free and adventurous in their undertakings. At other times, however, they can be self-indulgent and greedy. Their great strength is their single-minded drive to get the job done, and in extremes they can be fanatical.

Examples

Richard Gere, Dustin Hoffman, Michael Jackson, Kevin Keegan, Greta Scacchi, General Norman Schwarzkopf.

The Number 8 child

These children are best supported by their parents when they bring out their innate strengths through intellectual argument. They need to participate in debate and discussion on a whole range of issues at home and at school.

Number 8 children are harmed by over–indulgence. As the Youngest Son in *I Ching* symbolism they need to be encouraged to exert self-discipline and to help around the house. Having a Soil nature, they are confused and damaged by hypocritical behaviour on the part of parents or teachers.

The Number 9 character

These people are the brightest and liveliest of all the nine numbers. They tend to wear their heart on their sleeve and in many cases are extremely affectionate. They have a bubbly personality and come across as very inspiring – this 'fire' nature can provide 'illumination' to those around them. But they can also appear proud and vain, which may come across in their lifestyle, expression, private life and spontaneous expression. They also have a tendency to be self-centred.

They often act impulsively without having thought through the consequences of their actions, and though keen to initiate ideas are not necessarily the best at seeing them through. Of all the nine numbers they really do live in the moment. In many fields, the 9 Fire character can lead the way in terms of brilliance, genius, generosity and dedication.

Examples

John Cleese, Stephen Hawking, Hugh Hefner, Bob Hoskins, Jürgen Klinsmann, Rod Stewart.

The Number 9 child

These children are best supported by parents who can teach them consideration for others, how to develop patience, to plan and to see tasks through. The nature of these children can be spoilt if they are not given any discipline. Fire needs to be contained, and since this character can be very impulsive Number 9 children need order in their lives.

8

YOUR ENERGETIC NUMBER

Discovering the third number – your energetic number – completes the astrological chart using the 9 House system of astrology. In Western astrology it corresponds to the rising sign. This number shows how you appear to others in the world through your actions and the impressions that you give. If someone who did not know you particularly well was given the opportunity to describe you from brief encounters, this is how they would see you. For example, if your energetic number was 3 Tree your habits and behaviour would be driven primarily by the 3 Tree nature: active, outgoing, noisy and vibrant.

Later in the chapter you will be able to put your three numbers together and start to see what that combination can create. This is developed in detail in Chapter 9.

How to Discover Your Energetic Number

In Chapter 4 you discovered your principal number and in Chapter 7 your character number. You will need this information in order to determine your energetic number. Now look at the nine versions of the Magic Square set out opposite. As you go through the sequence you will see that each time the Magic Square rotates by one square in an anti-clock-

8	4	6
7	9	2
3	5	1

7	3	5
6	8	1
2	4	9

6	2	4
5	7	9
1	3	8

5	1	3
4	6	8
9	2	7

4	9	2
3	5	7
8	1	6

3	8	1
2	4	6
7	9	5

2	7	9
1	3	5
6	8	4

1	6	8
9	2	4
5	7	3

9	5	7
8	1	3
4	6	2

4	9	2
3	5	7
8	1	6

wise direction, the central number reduces by 1. Below these nine Magic Squares is the Magic Square of Bagua, which is the reference point for this whole system. It also appears as the central one of the nine versions laid out above it.

Find which one of the nine Magic Squares has your character (second) number in the centre. Also make a note of where your principal (first) number appears within that same Magic Square. Now see which House your principal number is occupying by referring to the Magic Square of Bagua at the bottom. This gives you your third or energetic number.

Here are some examples:

Examples:

4.6.?

5	1	3
4	6	8
9	2	7

Gives an energetic number of 3 and therefore a combination of 4.6.3.

2.5.?

4	9	**2**
3	5	7
8	1	6

Gives an energetic number of 2 and therefore a combination of 2.5.2.

8.2.?

1	6	**8**
9	2	4
5	7	3

Gives an energetic number of 2 and therefore a combination of 8.2.2.

8.9.?

8	4	6
7	9	2
3	5	1

Gives an energetic number of 4 and therefore a combination of 8.9.4.

5.5.?   3.3.?

4	9	2
3	**5**	7
8	1	6

2	7	9
1	**3**	5
6	8	4

Gives an energetic number of 5 and therefore a combination of 5.5.5.

Gives an energetic number of 5 and therefore a combination of 3.3.5.

Understanding Your Energetic Number

What follows is a list of the attributes that correlate with this energetic number, together with some examples. This is designed to help you to achieve a clearer and fuller picture of your chart using the 9 Star system of astrology.

1 Water

There are two types of 1 Water. Your expression could be passionate, sociable and very bubbly, like freshly oxygenated water. On the other hand, you could give the impression of being shy, cautious, indecisive and prone to procrastination.

Examples

Julie Christie, Liza Minnelli, Queen Victoria.

2 Soil

You will appear reserved, diplomatic and helpful. A reliable person who keeps their word, you are detail-minded and potentially fussy.

Examples

Michael Caine, Nigel Mansell, Pete Sampras.

3 Tree

The overall impression that you give is one of spontaneity. You have plenty of energy and great optimism, and are enthusiastic about whatever you take on. Your mode of expression is likely to be noisy and vivacious rather than quiet and retiring!

Examples

Richard Burton, Janis Joplin, Eva Peron.

4 Tree

You will appear quiet, dependable, gentle and helpful. You keep your word. The symbolism of Wind may give the impression that you are easily influenced by events around you. Of all the nine energetic types you have the greatest tendency towards change.

Examples

John Major, George Washington, Desmond Tutu.

5 Soil

Your energetic manner will certainly be noticed because it shows itself as a commanding and in some cases domineering presence. It is very important for you to be seen to be involved. The 5 Soil is merely emphasising the previous two numbers within your chart – that is to say, the number 5 brings out a very dominant quality in the preceding two numbers, which are inevitably the same.

Examples

Bob Geldof, George Bernard Shaw, Ike Turner.

6 Metal

The impression you give is of being straightforward and sincere, which can be direct and even overbearing at times. However, you are basically careful, prudent and organised. Your actions are clear and your behaviour predictable.

Examples

Rupert Murdoch, Laurence Olivier, Robespierre.

7 Metal

Your energetic nature is revealed to the world by your fun-loving, humorous manner. You enjoy your independence. Listening to others and making them feel at ease is your great skill. Your wit, charm and sense of humour are likely to form the strongest impression you leave with others.

Examples

Goldie Hawn, Diana, Princess of Wales, Burt Reynolds.

8 Soil

You are likely to give the impression that if there is a difficult way of doing things you will find it. You appear calm on the surface, which makes you seem shy. However, this is not so if you are provoked. One of your strongest tendencies is your persistence, even in the face of great challenges.

Examples

Eric Clapton, Damon Hill, J.W. von Goethe.

9 Fire

Your behaviour can be very ostentatious and flamboyant and you are naturally gregarious and sociable. You have a great tendency to be impulsive. Sometimes your deeper intuitive nature will shine through this energetic number.

Examples

Salvador Dali, Paul Gascoigne, Rudolph Valentino.

An astrological analysis of your family

Now that you have your full set of three astrological numbers you can start looking at this combination and making some comparisons. For instance, compare your numbers with those of your immediate family and see if a pattern emerges. Who do you share your principal number with? Whose character is the same as yours? Energetically, who would go about tasks or challenges in a similar way to you? Fill in the chart opposite with the numbers of family members and friends.

At the same time you can compare who you were as a child (your second or character number) in relation to your parents and siblings. Use the guidelines in Chapter 5 to determine what kind of relationship would have existed in childhood and whether that is any different now in adulthood. Equally, you could apply this exercise to colleagues at work.

Name	Principal number	Character number	Energetic number
Self			

Once you have done this, begin to look at:

- Who you related well to in your childhood
- Who you relate well to nowadays
- Where there has been conflict
- Where you have a similar outlook or mode of expression
- Where you give support
- Where you receive support

Very often in families these numbers recur time and time again. Using the Five Transformation diagram overleaf you could begin to observe where your principal, character or energetic number conflicts, supports or is supported by other numbers within the cycle. This is a fascinating and never-ending story. Remember that you were your second (character) number until you reached the age of 18, and that we all return to this nature when we are under pressure or are upset. We often find ourselves in situations of this kind within the family.

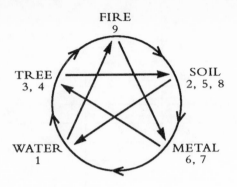

The British royal family

Name	Principal number	Character number	Energetic number
Queen Victoria	1	5	1
Queen Elizabeth the Queen Mother	1	3	3
Queen Elizabeth II	2	9	7
Princess Margaret	7	2	1
Prince Philip	7	4	8
Prince of Wales	7	8	4
Prince Andrew	4	8	1
Prince Edward	9	4	1
Princess Anne	5	5	5
Diana, Princess of Wales	3	1	7
Duchess of York	5	3	7
Prince William	9	1	4
Prince Harry	7	1	2

This example of a family very much in the public eye may help you gain insights into the relationships that could exist within your own family. It is interesting that the Queen Mother (1.3.3) and Queen Victoria (1.5.1) share the same principal number. Queen Elizabeth II (2.9.7) has as her principal number 2 Soil. If you recall, this represents the diplomat and the person who would be looking for win/win situations in both family and public life.

Diana, Princess of Wales (3.1.7) would potentially feel conflict from 6 or 7 Metal, which appears in the principal numbers of Prince Philip, Princess Margaret and the Prince of Wales. She shares her second number (1 Water) with both her sons, Prince William and Prince Harry, which would make for a close relationship with mutual understanding. The Duchess of York (5.3.7) shares the energetic number 7 with Diana and, being in the same age group, they may have similar interests and modes of expression.

The Prince of Wales and his father have very similar numbers; however, they are in opposition in the last two spaces – Prince Philip is 7.4.8 and Charles 7.8.4. This could be interpreted as having a similar outlook but very different forms of expression. It is interesting that Camilla Parker-Bowles (8.6.7), being an 8 Soil, supports Charles (7 Metal).

Princess Anne has extraordinary numbers (5.5.5), which show a tendency towards stubbornness and determination in her youth – that is, until the age of 18. However, in adulthood these numbers can be very powerful, as the individuals who have them are very determined and capable of enormous workloads and great responsibility.

Conclusion

Before moving on to the next chapters familiarise yourself with how to work out all three numbers, and keep practising so as to gain ever more insight into the interpretations of these combinations. Libraries are useful sources of biographies. If there are characters in history who interest you, find out their dates of birth and see if the material provided by this book so far ties up with your understanding of the character.

9

THE 81 COMBINATIONS

This chapter gives my interpretation of the 81 combinations of the three numbers, together with examples of well-known people both living and dead.

On page 23 there was a chart for establishing your principal number. Remember that the astrological year begins on 4 February, and if you were born between 1 January and 3 February you should refer to the House from the previous year. Once you have located the section on your principal number, look up your month of birth. Check carefully under the heading for each month to make sure that you are clear when it begins and ends; for example, June begins on 6 June and ends on 7 July.

1 Water

February

4 February to 5 March
1.8.7
You may appear to be fun, independent and easy-going; however, people close to you will know that you need time for yourself and time to retreat. You can be uncommunicative at times and need your own space. But although you may appear withdrawn, you have enormous hidden strengths.

Examples

Michael Jordan (17 February 1963), Sidney Poitier (20 February 1927), G.A. Rossini (29 February 1792).

March

6 March to 5 April
1.7.8
You have enormous reserves of strength and energy, but these will not be visible to people as you tend to hide them. You tend to learn from your difficulties, and these challenges reappear throughout your life. As people get close to you they will discover that you have a deep inner security, that you are reflective, fun and playful. People close to you will find you charming and you have a knack of making them feel at ease in your company.

Examples

Eric Clapton (30 March 1945), Lesley-Anne Down (17 March 1954), Henrik Ibsen (20 March 1828).

April

6 April to 5 May
1.6.9
Potentially, you have an interesting and powerful combination of numbers. Your outward appearance may be flamboyant, impulsive or ostentatious; however, the way you operate in relationships with others can be quite determined and forceful. You have a strong sense of pride and hate being criticised. At other times you crave your own space to dream and plan your next moves. Deep down there is hidden strength and a great capacity for adventure.

Examples

Catherine the Great (2 May 1729), Engelbert Humperdinck (2 May 1936), Roy Orbison (23 April 1936).

May

6 May to 5 June
1.5.1
You appear to be shy or cautious or indecisive in your actions, and tend to be withdrawn and quiet in your expression. As people get closer to you, however, they will discover that you can be quite bold and demanding in your relationships. You have great potential strength for overcoming difficulties, a strong will and an assertive nature that is often hidden from the world.

Examples

Dennis Hopper (17 May 1936), Priscilla Presley (24 May 1945), Queen Victoria (24 May 1819).

June

6 June to 5 July
1.4.2
Essentially your Water nature gives you a deep and brooding quality which hides an underlying spirit of adventure and strength. On the surface, people may find you tactful and helpful, reliable and fastidious in your work. However, when they get closer they find an emotional nature that can be stubborn or impulsive. This changeable nature is born out by the characteristic of 4 Tree in your second number.

Examples

Michael Caine (17 June 1927), Johnny Depp (9 June 1963), Ken Russell (3 July 1927).

July

8 July to 7 August
1.3.3
The Water nature in your chart gives you great potential for patience and diplomacy. You also have a flexible and easy-

going nature. However, your character can be expressive bordering on explosive, and you are not afraid of hard work. You are seldom shy and you bring great energy and spontaneity to all you do. Your enthusiasm is probably expressed best vocally in laughter, noise and conversation.

Examples

Queen Elizabeth the Queen Mother (4 August 1900), Nelson Mandela (18 July 1918), Brigitte Neilson (17 July 1963).

August

8 August to 7 September
1.2.4
You appear generally quiet, dependable and helpful. You have great capacity either to be influenced, or to influence others through your actions and beliefs. Your driving nature is your desire to support that which you consider fair and right. You may draw this quality from the philosophical properties of Water which make you appear quiet and brooding, but which are really hiding your great inner reserves and capacity for adventure.

Examples

Fidel Castro (13 August 1927), Whitney Houston (9 August 1963), Van Morrison (31 August 1945).

September

8 September to 8 October
1.1.5
The 5 Soil number in your chart brings two qualities to your personality. First, it is essential for you to feel involved in family, work and community situations. You can be central to projects and enjoy having your voice heard.

Secondly, the 5 Soil can accentuate the Water qualities in your chart. This means that you will draw heavily on your deep inner strength, your underlying philosophical nature and your capacity to build bridges. You have a strong adventurous spirit which you can use either in social situations or on your own.

Examples

José Feliciano (10 September 1945), Bob Geldof (5 October 1954), David Seaman (19 September 1963).

October

9 October to 7 November
1.9.6
This combination in your chart gives you potential for leadership. You appear sincere, organised and straightforward in your approach to life. The driving force of Water in your chart can bring out a spirit of adventure or a deep brooding quality which hides your reserves of strength. However, people close to you will find you inspiring, affectionate, impulsive and spontaneous. You sometimes tend to be self-centred and vain.

Examples

John Blashford-Snell (22 October 1936), Michael Lynagh (25 October 1963), Roger Moore (14 October 1927).

November

8 November to 7 December
1.8.7
See February (p.112).

Examples

Billy Graham (17 November 1918), Goldie Hawn (21 November 1945), Peter Schmeichel (18 November 1963).

December

8 December to 5 January
1.7.8
See March (p.113).

Examples

Chris Evert (21 December 1954), Diane Keaton (5 January 1946), Annie Lennox (25 December 1954).

January

6 January to 3 February
1.6.9
See April (p.113).

Examples

Rowan Atkinson (6 January 1955), Shirley Bassey (8 January 1937), Kevin Costner (18 January 1955).

2 Soil

February

4 February to 5 March
2.2.5
It is very important for you to be involved and to feel appreciated for the role you play, whether on the world stage, at a community level or within your family. Take care not to become too domineering where other people's opinions are concerned. Your underlying nature (2 Soil) is helpful, supportive and diplomatic. You are most fulfilled when you are involved in giving service to others. Others may find you too fastidious and you need to be careful not to become obsessed with detail.

Examples

Roger Daltrey (1 March 1944), Abraham Lincoln (12 February 1809), Axel Rose (6 February 1962).

March

6 March to 5 April
2.**1**.**6**
You come across as sincere, straightforward, organised and logical, working with care and prudence. Your driving force is your desire to support and help others, and you can be tactful and diplomatic when under pressure. However, your character is primarily driven by Water. Those close to you will find you cautious, with the potential to procrastinate. This Water nature can make you shy or undisciplined, but equally gives you the potential to be fun and sociable.

Examples

Bela Bartok (25 March 1881), Brian Clough (21 March 1935), Dame Vera Lynn (20 March 1917).

April

6 April to 5 May
2.**9**.**7**
Although your fundamental nature is consistent, helpful and supportive of others, many will find you very independent and fun-loving. Your energetic quality (7 Metal) gives you a charming, easy-going approach to life. Your Fire character will give rise to spontaneous outbursts of lively behaviour. You can be impulsive, affectionate and sometimes self-centred. Above all, when in full flow you can be an inspiration to those around you.

Examples

Dudley Moore (19 April 1935), Stuart Pearce (24 April 1962), Jacques Villeneuve (9 April 1971).

May

6 May to 5 June
2.8.8
In friendships and in business relationships you keep your word. You are consistent in what you do, supportive and helpful to those around you. Sometimes you can get fussy, even fanatical about detail. Your character and energetic nature are governed by 8 Soil, which at times can make you seem retiring and uncommunicative. But this quietness can change very quickly if you are provoked, and you are quite capable of coming out with very direct arguments. Overall, this is a very strong, reliable combination of the 9 House numbers.

Examples

Tony Blair (6 May 1953), Sir Norman Foster (1 June 1935), Michael Portillo (26 May 1953).

June

6 June to 7 July
2.7.9
People close to you will enjoy your witty and entertaining nature. You have a playful, fun-loving nature which is flexible and easy-going. Much of this comes from your deep sense of inner security. Basically, you have a diplomatic and helpful quality dedicated to the service of others. It is your outward expression (Fire) that can make you flamboyant or ostentatious and at times very impulsive. This fire nature also gives you a deep intuition and you are very capable of

'illuminating' those around you when they cannot see clearly what step to take next.

Examples

Benazir Bhutto (21 June 1953), Tom Cruise (3 July 1962), the Dalai Lama (6 July 1935).

July

8 July to 7 August
2.6.1
You have a very determined character that sees the world logically and clearly. You like to do things well or not at all. This reliable, prudent nature can be used powerfully in helping others in diplomatic situations, and you have great potential for leadership. On the surface, people may find you either shy, cautious and indecisive or, conversely, very sociable, bubbly and excitable.

Examples

Yul Bryner (11 July 1917), Robert Mitchum (6 August 1917), Donald Sutherland (17 July 1935).

August

8 August to 7 September
2.5.2
You may appear diplomatic, tactful, helpful, reserved and reliable, but your deeper nature is much more bold and demanding. It is only when your back is against the wall that your strong will and assertive nature can shine through. You are fundamentally powerful at overcoming difficulties in your life.

Examples

Macaulay Culkin (26 August 1980), Nigel Mansell (8 August 1953), Pete Sampras (8 August 1971).

September

8 September to 8 October
2.4.3
You give the impression of tremendous energy and enthusiasm. You can have a very expressive nature – often verbally – and are very spontaneous in your actions. These qualities override your character, which is very trusting of others. You need good support; emotionally you are prone to ups and downs and can act impulsively. Generally, the consistent, helpful and supportive quality of the 2 Soil character is at the helm.

Examples

Jacqueline Bisset (13 September 1944), Michael Douglas (25 September 1944), Topol (9 September 1935).

October

9 October to 7 November
2.3.4
First impressions can be deceptive: to many you will seem quiet, dependable, helpful, gentle, diplomatic and consistent. You can be fastidious over detail in your work and life. People close to you will discover your inner nature (3 Tree), which can be very expressive and at times explosive. The symbolism here is Thunder, which can come without warning and be awesome to those around you.

Examples

Marie-Antoinette (2 November 1755), Lester Piggott (5 November 1935), Oscar Wilde (16 October 1854).

November

8 November to 7 December
2.2.5
See February (p.117).

Examples

Danny De Vito (17 November 1944), Indira Gandhi (19 November 1917), King Hussein of Jordan (14 November 1935).

December

8 December to 5 January
2.1.6
See March (p.118).

Examples

Tracey Austin (12 December 1962), Kim Basinger (8 December 1953), Arantxa Sanchez Vicario (18 December 1971).

January

6 January to 3 February
See April (p.118).

Examples

Wolfgang Amadeus Mozart (27 January 1756), Anna Pavlova (31 January 1882), Rod Stewart (14 January 1945).

3 Tree

February

4 February to 5 March
3.5.3
You are hard-working and quite aggressively strong-willed, with an assertive nature that can be bold and demanding. If you do experience difficulties in your life, you have one of the strongest natures to overcome them. Friends and family see you as spontaneous and energetic, and find it difficult to

keep up with your ideas and enthusiasm. You can be very expressive, often speaking your mind before thinking through the consequences. It was possible that you were precocious as a child.

Examples

Robert Altman (20 January 1925), Barry Humphries (17 February 1934), Sam Peckinpah (21 January 1925).

March

6 March to 5 April
3.4.4
You have a very optimistic outlook on life, are very hard-working and seem to have an endless supply of energy and spontaneity. It is possible that you developed talent and independence at an early age. You appear to the world to be quiet, gentle and dependable. You have a helpful nature that is very trusting of others, which can sometimes be a problem. Your character can be emotional, sometimes appearing over-enthusiastic or impulsive and at other times stubborn and obstinate. Essentially you need good support from family, friends and colleagues.

Examples

John Major (29 March 1943), Michelangelo (6 March 1475), Vincent Van Gogh (30 March 1853).

April

6 April to 5 May
3.3.5
You enjoy taking a commanding or controlling interest in family, work or social situations. It is important for you to feel involved. You are hard-working and extremely sponta-neous in what you do, with plenty of vitality and energy for

the projects you set yourself. People close to you may find you emotionally explosive from time to time and may need to take a frequent 'weather check' on you.

Examples

André Agassi (29 April 1970), Shirley MacLaine (24 April 1934), Whigfield (11 April 1970).

May

6 May to 5 June
3.2.6
You have a very hard-working nature with plenty of vitality and spontaneity for new projects and ideas. You may find that your ideas are well ahead of your colleagues' and they may find you precocious in this sense. In relationships you are supportive and helpful, and eager to calm the waters in family misunderstandings. You appear organised and detail-minded, but some may find this excessive and be irritated by it. There is an honesty and directness in you that some find endearing and others overbearing.

Examples

Naomi Campbell (22 May 1970), Grace Jones (19 May 1952), Harold Robbins (21 May 1916).

June

6 June to 7 July
3.1.7
Not afraid to take on plenty of work or commitments, you have a lot of energy and vitality and are quite happy taking each day as it comes. In relationships you may appear cautious and philosophical, and your hidden depths of emotion are only expressed to those close to you. Outwardly you can appear extrovert, sociable and charming. You have a great

capacity to make people feel at ease by listening to them and acknowledging them. Some would describe you as easy-going, with an independent nature.

Examples

Diana, Princess of Wales (1 July 1961), Boy George (14 June 1961), Isabella Rossellini (18 June 1952).

July

8 July to 7 August
3.9.8
You tend to go about your business in a quiet way. You have enormous strength and frequently learn in life through dealing with difficulties. When provoked or excited you can be extremely spontaneous or impulsive. You are bubbly, lively and affectionate, sometimes self-centred, but equally deeply intuitive. These characteristics combine with a hard-working, energetic nature that is full of optimism, and you may well succeed early in your career.

Examples

Giorgio Armani (11 July 1934), Mick Jagger (26 July 1943), Robin Williams (21 July 1952).

August

8 August to 7 September
3.8.9
The driving force behind your nature is spontaneity and an enormous capacity to take on work. Your optimistic, energetic nature can be an inspiration to those around you. You can appear ostentatious or flamboyant in manner; you are often impulsive and are not afraid to show off. In your personal dealings with others they may find you at times uncommunicative, needing to retreat into your own space

to think or reflect. You have a deep sense of security and can be very single-minded in what you would like to achieve. When provoked, you can respond with very shrewd arguments.

Examples

General Norman Schwarzkopf (22 August 1934), Alan Shearer (13 August 1970), Patrick Swayze (18 August 1952).

September

8 September to 8 October
3.7.1
Possessing energy, strength and vitality to take on tasks, you are not afraid of hard work or of breaking new ground. You appear indecisive, quiet, withdrawn and cautious; you are quite prone to procrastination, and some may find you shy. However, once you feel at ease with people, and certainly among close friends, you are witty, entertaining, playful and fun-loving. There is a deep reflective nature within you that comes out in creativity or verbal expression.

Examples

Leonard Cohen (21 September 1934), Julio Iglesias (23 September 1943), Peter Sellers (8 September 1925).

October

9 October to 7 November
3.6.2
On the surface, people find you reserved and tactful. You are always eager to make helpful suggestions or to lend a hand; equally, you can appear to be fussy over small details. Your true character, however, is borne out when under pressure and this is the full force of Heaven (6 Metal). It can

make you a perfectionist, proud and determined in your efforts and straightforward in your expression. You are not afraid of hard work and have the energy to take on projects and see them through.

Examples

François Mitterrand (26 October 1916), Matthew Pinsent (10 October 1970), Margaret Thatcher (13 October 1925).

November

8 November to 7 December
3.5.3
See February (p.122).

Examples

Billie-Jean King (22 November 1943), Imran Khan (25 November 1952), Meg Ryan (9 November 1961).

December

8 December to 5 January
3.4.4
See March (p.123).

Examples

Gavin Hastings (3 January 1962), Ben Kingsley (31 December 1943), Maggie Smith (28 December 1934).

January

6 January to 3 February
3.3.5
See April (p.123).

Examples

Chuck Berry (15 January 1926), Joe Frazier (12 January 1944), Elvis Presley (8 January 1935).

4 Tree

February

4 February to 5 March
4.8.1
The combination of numbers here can give you a shy, retiring nature, and many will see you as cautious and indecisive. You may be prone to procrastination. Sometimes, however, you appear very bubbly, sociable and outgoing. People close to you will find you uncommunicative at times as you need to retreat into your 'cave'. You can be single-minded in whatever you take on, which may lead to obstinacy and fanaticism. But overall you have a trusting, steady, consistent nature with plenty of common sense.

Examples

Prince Andrew (19 February 1960), Kevin Keegan (12 February 1951), Rudolf Steiner (28 February 1861).

March

6 March to 5 April
4.7.2
In your immediate dealings with people you are reserved, tactful and diplomatic. You keep your word, are good at time-keeping and sometimes get caught up in minute detail. Where you feel safe and comfortable, with family and friends, you can be very witty and entertaining. Overall you have a steady, consistent nature which is trusting of those around you, and you can be very influential on others.

Examples

Marlon Brando (3 April 1924), Ivan Lendl (7 March 1960), Ayrton Senna (21 March 1960).

April

6 April to 5 May
4.6.3
You have a strong, outgoing personality which is very expressive, especially with words, and you are full of spontaneity and enthusiasm for life. People who know you well, however, will find another side to your character – serious, determined, reserved and logical. You are proud and self-critical and do not take criticism well. Essentially you are trusting of others, consistent and steady, and can bring influence to your sphere.

Examples

Jean-Paul Belmondo (9 April 1933), Lenin (22 April 1870), Ruby Wax (19 April 1951).

May

6 May to 5 June
4.5.4
You appear to the world as a dependable character who keeps their word. You have a gentle, helpful, trusting nature and can bring your influence to bear on situations in which you are involved. Friends and family will find a very different nature which also emerges when you are under pressure: assertive, bold and demanding. You have an enormous capacity to overcome difficulties through your strong will and determination.

Examples

Joan Collins (23 May 1933), Mike Oldfield (15 May 1951), Roberto Rossellini (8 May 1906).

June

6 June to 7 July
4.4.5
You need to feel involved in situations at work or at home, and are likely to take a commanding position if challenged. You should take care not to become too obsessive. Overall, your character and driving force are governed by the element 4 Tree (Wind), which makes you steady, consistent, trusting and full of common sense. You must avoid being too stubborn or too impulsive, and you may find you need to ask for support.

Examples

George Bush (12 June 1924), Steffi Graf (14 June 1969), Paul McCartney (18 June 1942).

July

8 July to 7 August
4.3.6
You appear to others to have a very direct and straightforward way of expression. You can be well organised, detail-minded and elegant in your presentation. Sometimes you are stubborn and overbearing. Although your principal quality is a steady, consistent, trusting nature, under pressure the explosive nature of Thunder will appear. With your back against the wall you will not hold back from free expression or sheer determination through hard work. If you do get into trouble you are very adept at talking your way out of it.

Examples

Harrison Ford (13 July 1942), Angelica Houston (8 July 1951), John Houston (5 August 1906).

August

8 August to 7 September
4.2.7
You have a strong, independent nature and value time and space for reflection. Your immediate expression is often charming. On the surface, you appear easy-going and flexible. In pressurised situations you will seek a win/win situation. You can be supportive, helpful and extremely tactful. Sometimes you can get caught up in detail, which can annoy those around you. Overall you have a steady, consistent, trusting nature and your ideas can be very influential on others.

Examples

Ingrid Bergman (29 August 1915), T.E. Lawrence (15 August 1888), Roman Polanski (18 August 1933).

September

8 September to 8 October
4.1.8
More distant observers may find you deep, quiet and inwardly strong – the strong, silent type. You tend to learn through your mistakes and keep yourself to yourself until provoked, when you can come forward with a strong argument. People who know you well find you cautious, philosophical and easy-going. You have plenty of common sense with a steady, consistent nature which is trusting of others. You have the potential to influence others in a quiet, solid fashion.

Examples

Charlton Heston (4 October 1924), Damon Hill (17 September 1960), Sting (2 October 1951).

October

9 October to 7 November
4.9.9
You have a very powerful combination of numbers that could make you very influential on others. Your steady, consistent driving force is somewhat overpowered by all the Fire present in your make-up. You can be very intuitive and have enormous capacity to 'illuminate' the obvious to those around you. You can be flamboyant, ostentatious and lively. You have plenty of spontaneity, and you need to guard against impulsive actions that are self-centred.

Examples

Josef Goebbels (29 October 1897), Bob Hoskins (26 October 1942), Diego Maradonna (30 October 1960).

November

8 November to 7 December
4.8.1
See February (p.128).

Examples

Billy Connolly (24 November 1942), Gary Lineker (30 November 1960), John Mayall (29 November 1933).

December

8 December to 5 January
4.7.2
See March (p.128).

Examples

Kenneth Branagh (10 December 1960), Frank Sinatra (12 December 1915), Stalin (21 December 1879).

January

6 January to 3 February
4.6.3
See April (p.129).

Examples

Peter Beardsley (18 January 1961), Paul Newman (26 January 1925), Terry Venables (6 January 1943).

5 Soil

February

4 February to 5 March
5.2.8
Your combination of numbers includes all three varieties of Soil. Your principal number 5 gives you great strength of will and an ambitious, materialistic nature. You have great capacity for self-preservation and overcoming difficulties. Your 2 Soil underlying character is supportive and helpful and likes to resolve situations at work and in the family diplomatically. You can be quite fastidious. On the surface you may appear quiet and withdrawn, but your real strength comes out if you are provoked.

Examples

Zsa Zsa Gabor (6 February 1923), John McEnroe (12 February 1959), Elizabeth Taylor (27 February 1932).

March

6 March to 5 April
5.1.9
You often appear to be impulsive or ostentatious. People will be drawn to your intuitive nature and you can be prone to showing off, either in style or in creative skills. However,

when people get to know you more closely your Water nature can be revealed. You can be cautious and philosophical, and at times withdrawn. Your deeper nature is to view the world from a broad perspective, and you do not share your immediate plans and schemes with those around you. Your principal strength lies with your 5 Soil nature, which gives you an ambitious, materialistic streak. You have enormous strength of will and are keen to be at the centre of all you do.

Examples

Albert Einstein (14 March 1878), Alec Guinness (2 April 1914), Marcel Marceau (22 March 1923).

April

6 April to 5 May
5.9.1
You need to be the centre of your work and family. It often takes you time to mature in your field of creativity. You have great strength and enormous willpower. You can be materialistic and ambitious in whatever field you choose. Your character is spontaneous and impulsive, often inspiring those around you with your affection and lively nature. You can be self-centred. People may get the impression that you are shy or cautious and indecisive – however, as the other numbers indicate, this is not your deeper nature.

Examples

Ryan O'Neal (20 April 1941), Omar Sharif (10 April 1932), Emma Thompson (15 April 1959).

May

6 May to 5 June
5.8.2
Your unique combination of numbers can make you controlling and demanding. Always central in family and social

life, you are ambitious, potentially materialistic and good at self-preservation. You may seem reserved and diplomatic, though often friendly and helpful, to those around you. Others may find you too fussy about small details. It is your underlying 8 character that is revealed to those close to you and when you are under pressure. Generally you appear shy, retiring and uncommunicative, but when provoked you can display enormous tenacity, especially in argument.

Examples

Bob Dylan (24 May 1941), Henry Kissinger (27 May 1932), Jeremy Paxman (11 May 1950).

June

6 June to 7 July
5.7.3
You have a deep sense of inner security which allows you to give the impression of being secure and laid back. Your sensitive, reflective nature can be borne out in your observations of the world. You can be entertaining, witty and charming. Your Tree nature gives the world the impression that you are very expressive, spontaneous and energetic. Your driving force is your inner strength, which enables you to overcome difficulties. You can be demanding, materialistic and bold.

Examples

Josie Lawrence (6 June 1959), Hugh Lawrie (11 June 1959), Mike Yarwood (14 June 1941).

July

8 July to 7 August
5.6.4
You appear dependable and helpful. Your manner and style are often gentle, quiet, unassuming and deeply trusting of

others. However, your inner character is revealed to those close to you and comes to the fore when you are under pressure. This can make you very reserved, determined, proud, even rigid. You can be very self-critical and are keen to do everything reliably and as perfectly as possible. You are potentially extremely ambitious and materialistic, with an enormous sense of self-preservation which helps you overcome difficulties.

Examples

Richard Branson (18 July 1950), Bruce Oldfield (14 July 1950), Wallis Simpson (19 July 1896).

August

8 August to 7 September
5.5.5
You have a fascinating combination of numbers: the triple 5 expresses the beginning and the end of a cycle. With your enormous capacity for initiation and determination you have an assertive nature that can be bold and demanding of others. You may find that you learn through difficulties and benefit from this experience in middle age. You need to feel involved: whether with family, work or immediate social community, it is important that you play a part. Others may naturally gravitate towards you for counsel, inspiration or help.

Examples

Princess Anne (15 August 1950), Magic Johnson (14 August 1959), Peter O'Toole (27 August 1932).

September

8 September to 8 October
5.4.6
The impression you give is one of sincerity and honesty. You have a very logical, organised way of going about

things. Beneath this nature lies the softer 4 Tree character, which needs the support of others and can make you more emotional, leading you to change your mind. You can be stubborn and impulsive in nature, and either influenced or very influential. Principally, you have enormous strength of will and the power to overcome all manner of difficulties. You are central to the lives of people around you.

Examples

Mahatma Gandhi (2 October 1869), Thor Heyerdahl (6 October 1914), Carrie Otis (28 September 1968).

October

9 October to 7 November
5.3.7
Your driving force is to be involved, whether with family or community or in your workplace. Despite any early problems in your life you have great powers of self-preser-vation and the strength of will to overcome difficulties. You can be ambitious and materialistic. Family and friends find you hard-working in all that you undertake. Under pressure you can be extremely expressive and potentially explosive (Thunder). Energetically your nature is fun, charming and easy-going, with a strong desire for indepen-dence.

Examples

Brian Adams (5 November 1959), Albert Reynolds (3 November 1932), the Duchess of York (15 October 1959).

November

8 November to 7 December
5.2.8
See February (p.133).

Examples

Jacques Chirac (29 November 1932), Field–Marshal Viscount Montgomery (17 November 1887), Pamela Stephenson (4 December 1950).

December

8 December to 5 January
5.1.9
See March (p.133).

Examples

Joan Armatrading (9 December 1950), Michael Schumacher (3 January 1969), Dionne Warwick (12 December 1941).

January

6 January to 3 February
5.9.1
See April (p.134).

Examples

Muhammad Ali (18 January 1942), Stephen Hawking (8 January 1942), Franz Schubert (31 January 1797).

6 Metal

February

4 February to 5 March
6.5.6
Your principal strength lies in your bold, consistent nature. You can be very direct and highly moral, and have enormous potential for leadership. You give the impression that

you are organised, logical and straightforward in your dealings. You can be elegant in your expression and taste in clothing. Sometimes you can be stubborn and overbearing, and those close to you may find you very egotistical and demanding. You have a strong will and a need to feel in control.

Examples

James Dean (8 February 1931), Mikhail Gorbachev (2 March 1931), Naomi James (2 March 1958).

March

6 March to 5 April
6.4.7
All 6 Metal people have a potential for leadership. You have a direct and moral nature which you can express boldly. Superficially you may appear charming, easy-going, fun and independent. Underneath, however, you can be changeable and emotional, with character swings from stubbornness to impulsiveness. You are trusting, and many trust you. In your childhood it was important for you to have enormous support.

Examples

Jack Kerouac (12 March 1922), Sharon Stone (10 March 1958), Lord Tebbit (29 March 1931).

April

6 April to 5 May
6.3.8
Your driving force is your strong, persistent nature. You can be very direct, clear and moral in your outlook. On the surface, people may find you reserved or quiet. Others may be curious as to why you go about your tasks in a difficult

way. Your inner character (3 Tree) is hard-working, optimistic and energetic. You can be very expressive and potentially explosive.

Examples

John Gielgud (14 April 1904), Jessica Lange (20 April 1949), William Wordsworth (23 April 1850).

May

6 May to 5 June
6.2.9
This combination of numbers can give you leadership potential. The bold, direct and consistent nature of 6 Metal combines well with your energetic nature of Fire. You may appear flamboyant and showy to the world, and often impulsive in your actions. However, your deeper nature makes you a natural diplomat with a desire to support and help those around you. You can be fastidious and detail-minded – but prone to get lost in that detail.

Examples

Paul Gascoigne (27 May 1967), Andrew Neil (21 May 1949), Franjo Tudjman (14 May 1922).

June

6 June to 7 July
6.1.1
You have the potential to influence, direct or lead others through your ideas or style. The presence of Water in your character and energetic nature can lead to two quite different personalities. On the one hand you may appear passionate, sociable, extrovert and bubbly. On the other hand you may be prone to procrastination and appear quiet, withdrawn, shy or cautious. You have unique skills

of tact and diplomacy within your family and immediate circle.

Examples

Hermann Hesse (2 July 1877), Nicole Kidman (21 June 1967), Prince (7 June 1958).

July

8 July to 7 August
6.9.2
You have potential for boldness and daring, and a very persistent nature which believes that things worth doing are worth doing well. In their dealings with you, many will find you tactful, helpful and reliable. Pushed to the limit or under fire, you can be very spontaneous and impulsive. You are lively, affectionate and potentially deeply self-centred. To those who know you well, you can be a real inspiration.

Examples

Freddie Laker (6 August 1922), Clive Sinclair (30 July 1940), Daley Thompson (30 July 1958).

August

8 August to 7 September
6.8.3
Your 6 Metal principal number gives you potential for leadership. You can be very direct, moral and consistent. On the surface you are expressive, energetic, enthusiastic and spontaneous. Those who know you well will appreciate your need to retreat into your 'Mountain': sometimes you will be shy, uncommunicative and deeply private. But if provoked you can come out with a strong argument or take the side of a cause that you feel is just.

Examples

Napoleon Bonaparte (15 August 1769), Richard Gere (21 August 1949), Shelley Winters (18 August 1922).

September

8 September to 8 October
6.7.4
Although you have the potential to lead and direct others, you appear gentle, quiet and helpful to those around you. You keep your word and are dependable. Your deep inner security gives the impression that you are reflective and laid back. You express yourself to those close to you in an entertaining, witty way. You have a great sense of humour and are playful.

Examples

Zandra Rhodes (19 September 1940), Archbishop Desmond Tutu (7 October 1931), Twiggy (19 September 1949).

October

9 October to 7 November
6.6.5
You have very powerful numbers that relate to leadership potential. You can be very determined and bold in what you wish to achieve, while at the same time logical, careful and prudent in your actions. You are naturally self-critical and it is important for you to do the job properly or not at all. You need to feel involved, whether with work, family or some social cause. You can take a controlling position and need to be careful not to appear too domineering or too obsessive.

Examples

Pelé (23 October 1940), Julia Roberts (28 October 1967), Sigourney Weaver (8 October 1949).

November

8 November to 7 December
6.5.6
See February (p.138).

Examples

Dr Christiaan Barnard (8 November 1922), Boris Becker (22 November 1967), Jamie Lee Curtis (22 November 1958).

December

8 December to 5 January
6.4.7
See March (p.139).

Examples

Willy Brandt (18 December 1913), King George VI (14 December 1895), Victoria Principal (3 January 1950).

January

6 January to 3 February
6.3.8
See April (p.139).

Examples

Placido Domingo (21 January 1941), Lisa Goddard (20 January 1950), Franz Schubert (31 January 1797).

7 Metal

February

4 February to 5 March
7.8.4
You have the potential to bring your accumulated wealth of experience to whatever you do. This can make you an

excellent listener and equally a very persuasive speaker. You are stylish, independent and charming. On the surface you may appear quiet, helpful, gentle and trusting – you keep your word. Your inner nature can sometimes be shy, retiring and uncommunicative. This 8 Soil character needs time to retreat and take stock of events. You can be tenacious, obstinate and single-minded in whatever you take on.

Examples

Cindy Crawford (28 February 1966), Antonio Vivaldi (4 March 1678), George Washington (22 February 1732).

March

6 March to 5 April
7.7.5
You have a deep sense of inner security which allows you to take on challenges without fear. Your wit and sense of humour reflect the way you experience life. You can be naturally charming – capable of both listening and making people feel at ease in conversation. Although you are intrinsically easy-going and flexible, you need to feel that you are in control in social and domestic situations. You have a commanding nature and need acknowledgement for your ideas and creative talents.

Examples

Chris Evans (1 April 1966), Ali McGraw (1 April 1939), Emile Zola (2 April 1840).

April

6 April to 5 May
7.6.6
You have a charming, stylish nature which lends itself well to your skills as a writer or orator. Your straightforward,

logical approach to life can be very sincere and persuasive to others. Deep down, you have a reserved and careful nature. Your manner and presentation can be direct, detailed and critical. You have the potential to lead through your charm and common sense.

Examples

David Beckham (2 May 1975), David Frost (7 April 1939), Michelle Pfeiffer (29 April 1957).

May

6 May to 5 June
7.5.7
You have the strength of character to overcome difficulties, especially as you mature. Your nature can be demanding, even aggressively so: you have a strong will and can be very assertive in what you want. On the surface you appear independent, fun and charming. Many will find you easy-going and unruffled by pressure. You can bring your accumulated experience of life to your writing or speaking. You have the great skill of making others feel at ease by listening to their point of view.

Examples

Zola Budd (26 May 1966), Thomas Hardy (2 June 1840), William Pitt the Younger (28 May 1759).

June

6 June to 7 July
7.4.8
You have a quiet, deep determination – the strong, silent type. But this nature can quickly change if you are provoked, and you are capable of strong, well thought out argument. You are at ease sharing your ideas, whether in

public or in private. Your independent nature can be borne out by your unique ideas or your go-it-alone lifestyle. Deep down, you have a trusting nature that can equally bring out trust in others concerning your ideas. You are capable of swings in your nature, and need to control your impulsiveness and stubbornness.

Examples

Prince Philip (10 June 1921), Enoch Powell (15 June 1912), Mike Tyson (30 June 1966).

July

8 July to 7 August
7.3.9
You have a very determined nature and are not afraid of hard work. You enjoy the pioneering side of projects. You are capable of being very expressive – sometimes explosive. You can be an inspiration to those around you, shining a light on the obvious. You bring your life experience to whatever you choose to do, and in combination with your articulacy this can make you a very persuasive speaker.

Examples

Peter Bogdanovich (30 July 1939), Sally Gunnell (29 July 1966), Cat Stevens (21 July 1948).

August

8 August to 7 September
7.2.1
Your deep reflective nature is most at ease with close friends. You are charming and have a natural gift for making those around you feel comfortable. The immediate impression you give is one of cautiousness and shyness. You

can be indecisive and prone to procrastination. Deep down, you are supportive, helpful and tactful. You are sensitive and care deeply for what is fair and right. Try not to get caught up in too much detail.

Examples

Gloria Estefan (1 September 1957), Stephen Fry (24 August 1957), Melanie Griffiths (9 August 1957).

September

8 September to 8 October
7.1.2
You are fun-loving, witty and charming. Your great skill lies in your capacity to make those around you feel listened to and acknowledged. Your insights are often direct and witty. Your 2 Soil nature makes you helpful and diplomatic in your immediate contact with others – you would make the perfect host. Your character can fluctuate from extrovert, sociable, fun-loving and undisciplined to quiet, withdrawn, cautious and philosophical.

Examples

Jeremy Irons (19 September 1948), Clive James (7 October 1939), Olivia Newton John (26 September 1948).

October

9 October to 7 November
7.9.3
You are not afraid of hard work, and have an energetic, enthusiastic quality that enjoys spontaneity in what you do. You enjoy breaking new ground and can be very inspiring to those around you. You do need to feel acknowledged and central to whatever you undertake. You have the capacity to express yourself well through composing,

writing or talking. Your views are principally expressed through your accumulation of life experience.

Examples

John Cleese (27 October 1939), Lulu (3 November 1948), Giuseppe Verdi (10 October 1813).

November

8 November to 7 December
7.8.4
See February (p.143).

Examples

Auguste Rodin (12 November 1840), Tina Turner (26 November 1939), the Prince of Wales (14 November 1948).

December

8 December to 5 January
7.7.5
See March (p.144).

Examples

Gérard Depardieu (27 December 1948), Sinead O'Connor (8 December 1968), Giacomo Puccini (22 December 1858).

January

6 January to 3 February
7.6.6
See April (p.144).

Examples

John Hurt (22 January 1940), Richard Nixon (9 January 1913), Boris Yeltsin (1 February 1931).

8 Soil

February

4 February to 5 March
8.2.2
You have a strong sense of justice. Single-minded and determined in whatever you take on, you are hard-working and learn through your own experience. You can be reserved in your expression, and have a natural flair for diplomacy. The double 2 Soil nature makes you very helpful and supportive in family, community and social issues.

Examples

Yasser Arafat (17 February 1929), Lord Baden-Powell (22 February 1857), George Frederick Handel (23 February 1685).

March

6 March to 5 April
8.1.3
You are strong and single-minded in whatever you take on. A sense of fair play and justice is important to you. Your actions are born out of contemplation and reflection rather than spontaneity. You are hard-working, enthusiastic and often pioneering in your creative skills. Your inner nature, which is revealed more with family and in relationships, is often cautious, philosophical and deep. To the outside world, you may appear shy.

Examples

Elton John (25 March 1947), Maurice Ravel (7 March 1875), Wyatt Earp (19 March 1848).

April

6 April to 5 May
8.9.4
Your driving force is your quiet, determined nature. You have great reserves of hidden strength and can be single-minded in whatever you choose to take on. On the surface, you will appear helpful, gentle, quiet and dependable, always keeping your word. However, when provoked you can be explosive, stubborn and self-centred. Your strength and energy can be an inspiration to those around you, but you need to avoid being too impulsive.

Examples

Alan Bond (22 April 1938), Glen Campbell (22 April 1938), Jeremy Thorpe (29 April 1929).

May

6 May to 5 June
8.8.5
It is easy for you to get deeply involved in family, work and social/community situations, when you tend to take on a controlling quality. Your principal driving force is your single-minded determination to ensure fair play. There are times when you may appear shy, retiring and uncommunicative, but this image changes rapidly when you need to express your opinion. It is then that your qualities of single-mindedness and tenacity become fully expressed; you need to guard against being fanatical in what you do.

Examples

Brian Eno (15 May 1947), Pope John Paul II (18 May 1920), Brooke Shields (31 May 1965).

June

6 June to 7 July
8.7.6
You can appear disarmingly honest and straightforward. You have a logical and organised approach, are naturally elegant and appreciate the arts. Your principal driving force is your single-minded determination, which can best express itself concerning what is fair and just in the world. Friends and family will find you flexible, easy-going, entertaining and witty. You are naturally charming and have the skill of making those around you feel at ease.

Examples

John Constable (11 June 1776), Jerry Hall (2 July 1956), Salman Rushdie (19 June 1947).

July

8 July to 7 August
8.6.7
Your principal nature is your quiet, strong, single-minded determination: you achieve success through sheer hard work. On the surface you can appear easy-going and fun. You can be charming, and have the potential to make those around you feel at ease. Your underlying character of 6 Metal gives you a very direct, bold nature. You are very clear in what you believe in and very direct in your mode of expression. You have immense pride and are particularly self-critical, so you do not take criticism from others well. It is important for you to accomplish all that you undertake with skill, prudence and logic.

Examples

Tom Hanks (9 July 1956), Arnold Schwarzenegger (30 July 1947), O.J. Simpson (9 July 1947).

August

8 August to 7 September
8.5.8
You do not learn things easily through academic or intellectual means – most of what you learn comes from your own life experiences and mistakes. You have enormous reserves of hidden strength and can appear uncommunicative until provoked. Your underlying character, 5 Soil, brings out an assertive and demanding nature. You have enormous potential for overcoming difficulties and challenges, which often become easier in middle age. There is a tendency towards control in your character, and it is important for you to be listened to.

Examples

Ronnie Biggs (8 August 1929), Johann Wolfgang von Goethe (28 August 1749), Keith Moon (23 August 1947).

September

8 September to 8 October
8.4.9
You are very resilient and capable of withstanding many of life's knocks. Your strong, determined single-minded nature is best borne out when you are fighting for what you feel is fair and right. You can appear impulsive and ostentatious in your behaviour. Others will benefit deeply from your intuition. Your inner character can be quiet and changeable, like the Wind. You need support from those around you and can be equally influential or influenced by others.

Examples

Betty Boothroyd (8 October 1929), Meatloaf (27 September 1947), Micky Rourke (16 September 1956).

October

9 October to 7 November
8.3.1
You achieve success in life through sheer strength of will and single-mindedness. You have enormous reserves of strength which allow you to overcome most difficulties. On the surface you can seem shy, quiet and cautious, and sometimes you are indecisive. However, when your back is to the wall you can throw yourself into hard work. Again, under pressure you can be very expressive to the point of explosion.

Examples

Derek Jacobi (22 October 1938), Ann Jones (17 October 1938), Martina Navratilova (18 October 1956).

November

8 November to 7 December
8.2.2
See February (p.149).

Examples

José Carreras (5 December 1947), Eddie Irvine (10 November 1965), Grace Kelly (12 November 1929).

December

8 December to 5 January
8.1.3
See March (p.149).

Examples

Will Carling (12 December 1965), Edward G. Robinson (12 December 1893), Steven Spielberg (18 December 1947).

January

6 January to 3 February
8.9.4
See April (p.150).

Examples

Princess Caroline of Monaco (23 January 1957), Carol Channing (31 January 1921), George Forman (22 January 1948).

9 Fire

February

4 February to 5 March
9.5.9
The powerful presence of Fire in your chart gives you clarity, brilliance and potential genius. You have the capacity to 'illuminate' those around you with your vision and ideas. Your sensitive nature needs acknowledgement from those around you, otherwise you lack confidence. Your behaviour can be impulsive and ostentatious, which can hide a deep intuitive nature. Your character is very strong-willed and you can be bold and demanding. You need to feel in control and have tremendous reserves to overcome difficulties and challenges.

Examples

Matt Dillon (18 February 1955), Greg Norman (10 February 1955), Voltaire (20 February 1694).

March

6 March to 5 April
9.4.1
You may appear from time to time cautious, quiet, withdrawn, perhaps even shy. You can be prone to procras-

tination. However, you are driven by a deep Fire nature which can give you great clarity and sensitivity. You are capable of inspiring those around you. You do need acknowledgement, and must not allow any lingering self-doubt. Your underlying character is emotional – sometimes stubborn, sometimes impulsive. You are very capable of being influenced by or, conversely, influencing others.

Examples

Johann Sebastian Bach (21 March 1685), Liza Minnelli (12 March 1946), Bruce Willis (19 March 1955).

April

6 April to 5 May
9.3.2
On the surface you can appear reserved, tactful and diplomatic. You can be fussy and fastidious over detail. Your principal driving force, however, is Fire, which can give you tremendous strength, clarity, vanity, sensitivity and brilliance. Under pressure you can be extremely expressive and emotionally explosive. You are not afraid of hard work.

Examples

Joanna Lumley (1 May 1946), Jack Nicholson (27 April 1937), Baron von Richthofen (the Red Baron, 2 May 1892).

May

6 May to 5 June
9.2.3
You are a very spontaneous and energetic person, with great enthusiasm especially for new projects that require a pioneering nature. You are not afraid to express yourself. Your principal nature is Fire, which can give you strength,

brilliance (bordering on genius), clarity and sensitivity. You are prone to vanity and need acknowledgement, otherwise you can lose confidence. Deep down, however, you are helpful, supportive and trusting.

Examples

George Best (22 May 1946), Eva Peron (7 May 1919), Debra Winger (17 May 1955).

June

6 June to 7 July
9.1.4
You can appear very beguiling and influential. You have an adaptable nature and trust your intuition. You are driven by your principal nature of Fire, which can make you vain, sensitive and brilliant. You are capable of leadership and inspiration. However, your inner character is Water, which can make you cautious or isolated under pressure. You need the support and acknowledgement of friends and family when you face a difficulty or crisis.

Examples

Che Guevara (14 June 1928), Tom Stoppard (3 July 1937), Donald Trump (14 June 1946).

July

8 July to 7 August
9.9.5
You have a strong desire to be involved, whether in family, work or community situations. Sometimes this can lead you to taking control, with a tendency to be domineering. You are driven by Fire, which can make you spontaneous and impulsive in your actions: you are lively, bubbly and affectionate, and can be deeply inspiring to those around you.

You can be sensitive and clear and are capable of showing others what is obvious to you. Try to avoid being too self-centred.

Examples

Stanley Kubrick (26 July 1928), Helen Mirren (11 July 1946), Iris Murdoch (15 July 1919).

August

8 August to 7 September
9.8.6
You have great potential for leadership, especially in the areas of what is fair, just or right in your opinion. Your manner can be sincere, direct, even overbearing. Your principal driving force is Fire, which gives you great strength, vanity, clarity and brilliance – a brilliance capable of illuminating stagnation around you. Deep down, you can be shy or retiring from time to time. When under pressure you can express powerful arguments, being almost fanatical in your beliefs.

Examples

Bill Clinton (19 August 1946), Freddie Mercury (5 September 1946), Mother Teresa (26 August 1910).

September

8 September to 8 October
9.7.7
You can be very charismatic and are not afraid to speak your mind, based on your own experience. You have an inner sense of security that can make you appear easy-going. You can be entertaining and witty, and have the potential for a great sense of humour. Your ideas can be inspiring and influential because you express them so clearly. You have a tendency towards vanity.

Examples

Barbara Castle (6 October 1910), Susan Sarandon (4 October 1946), Oliver Stone (15 September 1946).

October

9 October to 7 November
9.6.8
Your natural tendency is to learn through life's experiences rather than academically or through the advice of others. You can appear quiet and determined, but can become stubborn or argumentative when provoked. Your principal nature makes you powerful, vain and brilliant. On a deeper level you are very clear, self-critical and constantly on the look-out for perfection; you do not take criticism well.

Examples

Charles Dance (10 October 1946), Franz Liszt (22 October 1811), Tatum O'Neal (5 November 1955).

November

8 November to 7 December
9.5.9
See February (p.154).

Examples

Winston Churchill (30 November 1874), Keith Michell (1 December 1928), Monica Seles (2 December 1973).

December

8 December to 5 January
9.4.1
See March (p.154).

Examples

Marianne Faithfull (29 December 1946), Anthony Hopkins (31 December 1937), Rudyard Kipling (30 December 1865).

January

6 January to 3 February
9.3.2
See April (p.155).

Examples

David Bowie (8 January 1947), Mel Gibson (3 January 1956), Kate Moss (16 January 1974).

10

9 STAR KI AND SEXUALITY

Understanding our sexuality using 9 Star Ki astrology is another fascinating aspect of this subject. In Chapter 4 you discovered your principal character and read about the eight other characters. You will recall that, leaving aside 5 Soil, the remaining eight characters are divided into male and female qualities: 1, 3, 6 and 8 represent Middle Son, Eldest Son, Father and Youngest Son respectively, while 2, 4, 7 and 9 represent Mother, Eldest Daughter, Youngest Daughter and Middle Daughter respectively. The number 5 Soil (which has no trigram or family member) is influenced primarily by your second number (character), which you discovered in Chapter 7. Therefore, if your principal number is 5 Soil, in order to determine whether it is male or female you need to refer to your second number; for instance 5.4 = female, because number 4 is the Eldest Daughter. If your character number is 5, it takes the gender of your principal number.

Your principal number relates to your deeper sense of sexual security – how well at ease you are with your own sexuality. If this number is in line with your own gender it can give you both a deeper and an outward sense of security. However, if your principal number is opposite to your own gender you may find members of the opposite sex more challenging.

Your character (second) number represents the way you express yourself sexually in a more overt, superficial manner. This could relate to how you dress, how you go about attracting a partner and how confident you appear to the world in your relationships. When this number is in line with your own gender you often over-emphasise your maleness or femaleness in the way you dress or express yourself. When your character number is opposite to your own gender you have the potential to understand and relate deeply to members of the opposite sex without the necessity for any deep sexual attraction.

The Nine Principal Characters and Their Sexuality

To begin with, let's look at the fundamental qualities of the nine principal characters and relate this to their sexuality.

1 Water (male – Middle Son)

Of all the nine numbers, the dominance of Water in your make-up gives you the deepest sense of sexual energy. In Chinese medicine Water controls the function of the kidneys, bladder and reproductive system. Your sexual character can have two different interpretations, since in the natural world, water can be either bubbly, fresh and sparkling or deep, quiet and potentially stagnant.

You may therefore be potentially shy, cautious and indecisive about entering into a sexual relationship. You may find yourself celibate for long periods of your life. The image you may give the world is that of the wall-flower. However, underlying this cautious nature you have potentially very strong sexual feelings that are waiting to be expressed within a secure relationship. You can be adventurous with a partner and at the same time deeply loyal.

Water's nature can alternatively appear undisciplined. Imagine pouring a glass of water across a table – it would flow in every direction and you would have great difficulty in persuading it to return to the glass! Expressed in sexual terms this could mean you are too passionate, flirtatious and superficially sexy, having several relationships at the same time.

The symbolism of Middle Son within your chart gives you the potential to be a great 'listener' to your partner. The diplomatic nature of the Middle Son expresses itself well through your ability to hear your partner's needs and to communicate your own at the same time. The role of the Middle Son in the family is to create harmony through communication, and this quality expresses itself well within a sexual relationship as open communication.

Examples

Ursula Andress, Gina Lollobrigida, Burt Reynolds.

2 Soil (female – Mother)

If a woman has 2 Soil as her principal number it brings out the full force of femininity and mothering in the relationship. In a man it would also bring out mothering qualities, which you may find charming or not. This is the equivalent in the Western astrological system of a man having the influence of Cancer strongly in his make-up.

You will appear somewhat reserved sexually, but in a relationship you will be very reliable and supportive. Your deeper nature is to be of service to others, and this can be borne out in a relationship as well.

As a 2 Soil you will be potentially very loyal in a relationship. But you can have a tendency to be fussy and fastidious over some aspects of your relationship, which may irritate your partner. You also have the potential to be too dependent on your partner which may lead to disharmony.

The 2 Soil character is renowned for generosity, but you need to have this quality reciprocated or you will feel drained and used.

Examples

Kim Basinger, Tom Cruise, Marilyn Monroe.

3 Tree (male – Eldest Son)

With 3 Tree as your principal number you have the strongest sexual libido of all nine numbers. The 3 Tree nature represents the full force of spring breaking out of the depths of winter. The symbolism of Tree in this respect corresponds to virility and strength. You have the greatest potential for spontaneity in a sexual relationship, and can be very expressive and energetic. Of all the nine numbers you have the most potential to be preoccupied with the importance of sex in a physical sense.

The *I Ching* trigram for the Eldest Son represents the ground-breaking member of the family. The Eldest Son is traditionally precocious, optimistic and eager to explore. This nature can express itself within a relationship as spontaneity and the desire to explore different methods of lovemaking. The precocious nature of the Eldest Son can also translate into exploring your own sexuality at a young age and having your first sexual encounter much earlier than your peers.

Examples

Meg Ryan, Claudia Schiffer, Patrick Swayze.

4 Tree (female – Eldest Daughter)

The 4 Tree nature evokes the image of the full maturing of spring – the blossoming, dynamic force that we feel before the arrival of summer. The corresponding element in the *I*

Ching is Wind. Here, your sexual nature can have all the dynamism symbolic of spring, combined with an emotional, changeable nature that is represented by the wind.

You have a deeply trusting nature which, in combination with your spontaneity and changeable nature, can make you very impulsive in a sexual relationship. You can, for instance, be strongly attracted to someone and want to embark on a sexual relationship immediately. In the same way that you have a deep sense of trust in others, you give out to others a sincere and trusting quality. It is not uncommon for the 4 Tree to have experienced many relationships before finding satisfaction. The best advice is always to take time and ask your best friend for their opinion before you throw yourself into a new relationship. It is also very important to have the support and trust of your partner.

Examples

Angelica Houston, John Kennedy Jnr, Michael York.

5 Soil (male/female – Centre)

Being at the centre of this system of astrology, it is not difficult for you to put yourself at the centre of any relationship. It is important for you to maintain control in a sexual relationship. You can be domineering and demanding, and are quite capable of asserting yourself and being bold or unusual in your demands. Being at the centre, you can relate well to any of the other eight characters. This can either make you very compassionate and caring in the relationship, or demanding. If you have a soft, quiet nature you may find that too many demands are made of you, or you may become too dependent on your partner for your sexual satisfaction.

You could find yourself involved in unusual relationships, for example your partner may be a lot older or younger than yourself. Or your partner may be frequently unavailable due to other commitments or living or working a long way away. Given that the 5 Soil is at the centre, it is not uncommon to find yourself in a triangle situation.

Sex is important to you, and as a number 5 Soil you need to find a partner with the same degree of enthusiasm and a willingness to let you take control. At the same time, you need to develop patience and learn to listen to the desires of your partner.

Examples

Nick Nolte, Wallis Simpson, Elizabeth Taylor.

6 Metal (male – Father)

Having the full force of heaven/male/father/metal as the principal driving force in your sexuality can be an appealing and powerful quality for a man. However, if you are a woman this may make you too authoritative and dominant in the relationship. As a 6 Metal you are renowned for your strength, boldness and consistency, and have a great sense of trust in your partner.

Sex for a 6 Metal can be very straightforward, almost conservative – your reserved nature can make you perhaps the least adventurous of all the nine characters. It is, however, important for you to receive acknowledgement from your partner. Any criticism of your 'performance' can be devastating – as a 6 Metal you are well known for self-criticism, and that is sufficient. Your pride and desire for perfection mean that you take your time before choosing a partner, and when you have done so you are likely to remain loyal in a lasting, stable relationship. The full force of heaven in your chart can make you very direct about what you want and do not want, and you are likely to make clear distinctions about what you feel is morally right or wrong.

Examples

Richard Gere, Nicole Kidman, Sharon Stone.

7 Metal (female – Youngest Daughter)

As the Youngest Daughter of the *I Ching* family you have learnt from your older brothers and sisters. This gives you a deep sense of inner security within relationships, combined with a fun-loving nature. Your charming, sensitive nature makes you very responsive to your partner: you have a great capacity to listen and a desire to give him or her pleasure. You may appear flirtatious and playful to the world, and can easily hide your reflective qualities.

Your fun-loving, independent nature makes it difficult for you to make a long-term commitment. Having a partner who looks good and is stylish and equally fun-loving is important to you. When a sexual relationship becomes stagnant you may not have the patience to work on it, and move on instead.

Examples

Cindy Crawford, Michelle Pfeiffer, Kiefer Sutherland.

8 Soil (male – Youngest Son)

You bring strong energy and power to a sexual relationship. You have a deep, reflective nature and your partner may find you shy, retiring and uncommunicative at times: this is part of your desire to retreat into yourself. The symbolism of the appropriate trigram is Mountain, which means strength and stability and a need to retreat into your 'cave'.

You can be single-minded about what you want, self-indulgent and tenacious. Your partner may find you overbearing and obstinate from time to time. Initially your partner may be attracted by your quiet, strong, energetic quality, but may be offended when he or she provokes or chides you and you display a defensive or argumentative side not shown before.

As an 8 Soil you typically learn through your mistakes and successes. It is this accumulation of wisdom that can enrich the sexual relationship for both you and your partner. Try to communicate your own needs and listen more to your partner's needs.

Examples

Ry Cooder, Jerry Hall, Bianca Jagger.

9 Fire (female – Middle Daughter)

The presence of Fire in your chart makes you the most passionate of the nine characters. This Fire nature makes you very attractive to others, and your flamboyant nature is frequently misunderstood as flirting. You are naturally bubbly, lively, warm and affectionate. It is important for you to have your emotions, desires and feelings fully expressed within a sexual relationship. You can be very spontaneous and impulsive with your partner. You may initially be attracted by your partner's physique, eyes or even mannerisms. You also possess a deeply intuitive and sensitive nature and are quite capable of communicating what you want and listening to your partner's needs.

It is important for you to receive acknowledgement in your relationship. When criticised or jilted, you can become very depressed and introverted. This can also manifest in an enormous lack of confidence and a dark period of self-doubt. In these situations it is important for friends to help lift your spirits and bring out once again all your warmth and affection.

Examples

Cher, Sigmund Freud, Susan Sarandon.

Your Gender Relative to Your Astrology

You can now take a deeper look at your sexuality based on the gender of your principal number and your character number. To remind you of the gender of these numbers, take a look at the chart below which is based on the *I Ching* family members that the trigrams represent.

1 ☵	Water	Male	Middle Son
2 ☷	Soil	Female	Mother
3 ☳	Tree	Male	Eldest Son
4 ☴	Tree	Female	Eldest Daughter
5	Soil	Take on the gender of your other number e.g. if you are male and your numbers are 3.5 the 5 will take on the gender of the first number (male)	
6 ☰	Metal	Male	Father
7 ☱	Metal	Female	Youngest Daughter
8 ☶	Soil	Male	Youngest Son
9 ☲	Fire	Female	Middle Daughter

There are four possible combinations of your principal and character numbers. Below are some interpretations of these combinations, together with examples of individuals who share them. You may find that the combinations can shine a light on current or past relationships.

Principal number same gender/character number same gender

This can be a powerful combination for establishing a confident understanding and expression of your own sexuality.

Having both your deeper and surface nature in line with your gender makes you fully at ease with who you are. Being 'all male' or 'all female' can give you all the traditionally understood traits of your gender. For a man this may mean presenting yourself as macho man, strong and sexually confident. For a woman you could appear sensual and very feminine.

In the same way that the trigram for earth (three broken lines) and that for heaven (three bold lines) are traditionally viewed as the archetypal expressions of female and male energy respectively, you may have a somewhat idealistic view of relationships and sex. Your search for a partner may therefore take you a long time. You may have strong views about what you want from a relationship, and sometimes you will be disappointed when your partner does not match up to your ideal. Deep down you are comfortable with your own gender and sexuality, so you have no need to achieve sexual satisfaction all the time. You may go through long periods of celibacy, which are not a challenge for you. You are quite prepared to wait for the 'right person'.

Because you are secure and comfortable in your sexuality you like to make good friends of the opposite sex. However, because you lack the opposite gender in your make-up you may not fully understand them.

Examples

Joan Collins (4.5), James Dean (6.5), Jodie Foster (2.2), Zsa Zsa Gabor (5.3), Tom Jones (6.1), Burt Reynolds (1.8).

Principal number opposite gender/character number opposite gender

This combination can be a challenge, as you lack your own gender in either your principal or character number. On a deeper level this can leave you insecure in your sexuality, which, rather than make you lose any interest in sex, tends to have the opposite effect – you can become almost obsessed with it. This obsession can give you tremendous libido, but the lack of gender in your principal and character numbers may lead to dissatisfaction with sex itself.

Any obsession with sex can manifest in a number of ways – for example, you may have a deep-seated and unjustified fear of the opposite sex. As a result you may want to take advantage of the opposite sex by not committing yourself to a relationship or by using your partner for your own satisfaction. Because of your own insecurity you are unlikely to be taken advantage of and are more likely to be on the defensive. It is possible that you could exploit the opposite sex, blame them or have difficulty in trusting them. Although you are fundamentally independent by nature, in your search for your sexual identity you may find role models from your own gender and may try to live up to some idealised view of what a man or woman should be.

Examples

Warren Beatty (9.4), Catherine Deneuve (3.6), Diana, Princess of Wales (3.1), Britt Ekland (3.8), Sigmund Freud (9.2), Hugh Hefner (2.9).

Principal number opposite gender/character number same gender

During your adolescence, when your character number was the driving force of your personality, it would have been in line with your gender. Therefore at that age you may have been very confident with the opposite sex, finding them non-threatening and being totally at ease with them. But as you approached the age of 18 and began to move into the influence of your principal number you may have come to misunderstand or mistrust the opposite sex.

When you are an adult your gender appears on the surface of your nature. This may result in you emphasising your maleness or femininity in your outward expression, which could mean the way you dress or the way you communicate. When your own gender appears on the surface through your character, it is harder for you to relate to members of the opposite sex, who may feel threatened by your superficial masculinity/femininity. With your principal number opposite your own gender this can leave you feeling very insecure about your sexuality on a deeper level.

Despite these challenges, of all four combinations you have the greatest potential for an objective understanding of other people's relationships and sexuality. Having both combinations within your chart gives you great intuition and insight into others' lives. However, it is difficult for you to apply this depth of understanding to your own situation.

Examples

Brigitte Bardot (3.7), Bill Clinton (9.8), Greta Garbo (5.4), Hugh Grant (4.1), Whitney Houston (1.2), Sylvester Stallone (9.1).

Principal number same gender/character number opposite gender

This combination gives you a very even keel in understanding your own sexuality, and a clear insight into members of either sex. Your surface nature is opposite to your gender, so when members of the opposite sex encounter this in their immediate dealings with you they will feel very comfortable and unthreatened. Your deep understanding of the opposite sex, which is borne out by your character number being the same as theirs, can put you into a great position of trust or confidence. You have the capacity to be an excellent counsellor, friend or listener to members of the opposite sex. But this feeling of confidence and natural ease with the opposite sex can be misunderstood as a sexual advance.

Since your principal number is the same as your gender,

and the principal number always relates to our deeper sexual identity, you may at times be unable to express your emotions easily. Of all the four combinations, you are probably the hardest to get to know on this level. However, this side of your nature is not immediately apparent to members of the opposite sex, as you are so much at ease with them through having your character number in line with their gender.

Examples

Farrah Fawcett (9.3), Mick Jagger (3.9), Marilyn Monroe (2.8), Roger Moore (1.9), Ken Russell (3.9), Mae West (9.8).

The double 5 Soil

Since 5 Soil does not have a trigram within the *I Ching* it takes on the gender of the other number when we look at our principal or character number. However, individuals whose combination is 5.5.5 take on the gender of their own sex.

Examples

Peter O'Toole (5.5), Rocky Marciano (5.5), Mary Shelley (5.5).

11

YEARLY PREDICTIONS

The preceding chapters have dealt essentially with 'who' you are. The next three chapters are going to deal with 'where' you are. As you have already discovered, you have much in common with people born 9, 18, 27 (and so on) years before or after you. In other words, you were all born at the same time within a nine-year cycle.

Try to imagine your life revolving in these nine-year (and nine-month) cycles. This could be graphically represented as a star making an elliptical orbit around the sun that took nine years. There would be times during that nine-year orbit when the star was close to the sun. If you were that star, at such times your natural Ki would feel highly charged, active and noticed. Then imagine being at the point in the orbit which was furthest away from the sun – you would naturally feel cooler, quieter and more withdrawn, and there would be less of a charge of Ki energy. If you were at a point in the orbit approaching the sun, this could represent the rising energy of spring, and your Ki would be evolving and planning the future. If, on the other hand, you were at a point in the orbit when you were leaving the heat of the sun and moving towards the cooler, darker aspects of the orbit, you would tend to consolidate and conserve your energy.

The Benefits of this Information

Knowing where you are at any given time within the nine-year or nine-month cycle can save you from frustration or disappointment. You can also use this information wisely to plan the timing of new projects, moving house, changing jobs or studying. It can make an enormous difference to the outcome of our planned ventures if we can choose an appropriate time.

Ancient Chinese imagery and symbolism regarding the *I Ching*, Feng Shui and 9 House astrology was primarily drawn from people's observation of nature. Living in a climate with four distinct seasons can give us a clearer understanding of this cycle. China has always been a predominantly agricultural country. If, using this system, a year or month was seen to be governed by the element 1 Water, farmers would have taken on board the idea that the weather in that year or month would be damper than usual. As a result, they may have chosen to plant crops that preferred these wetter conditions. Advisers of rulers and community-leaders would have taken into account not just the dominant number that represented the year involved but the place where the ruler or leader 'sat' within the Magic Square that that year represented. In this way the individual learnt the most auspicious time to begin, to resolve, to travel or to consolidate.

The system that was used thousands of years ago can still have value for us today. If the Ki energy is with you when you make an undertaking, it is far easier to achieve success. Choosing the right time to make a journey can save a lot of trouble and missed opportunities. Setting out when the Ki energy is against you or stagnant can put obstacles in your path.

The exciting and somewhat paradoxical nature of this system is that it is not always beneficial. For example, when you are occupying the House of 9, which you can broadly interpret as meaning that you are in the limelight, you may well expect fame and fortune. It is all to do with exposure – not only will your surface Ki energy be noticed by others, but so will what you have been doing in the recent past. The project or scheme that you have been working on so hard could now be recognised. Your hard work and dedication in the office may at last be acknowledged and appreciated by your boss. Equally, however, areas of your life that you have wished to conceal or to remain private can become exposed. These interpretations of the 9 Houses will be dealt with later in this chapter.

How Does It Work?

The first thing you need to know when understanding 'where' you are within the nine phases of this cycle is 'who' you are. For this you need to know your principal number (refer to pp. 22–4 if you do not already know it). Remember also that you can use the chart on p. 23 to discover what number controlled a particular year in history. For example, a quick glance will reveal that 1941 was governed by the house of 5 Soil – in other words, 5 Soil was at the centre of the Magic Square at that time.

If you look at the nine squares overleaf you will notice a pattern through which the number 3 moves.

1	6	8
9	2	4
5	7	**3**

Fig 1

9	5	7
8	1	**3**
4	6	2

Fig 2

8	4	6
7	9	2
3	5	1

Fig 3

7	**3**	5
6	8	1
2	4	9

Fig 4

6	2	4
5	7	9
1	**3**	8

Fig 5

5	1	**3**
4	6	8
9	2	7

Fig 6

4	9	2
3	5	7
8	1	6

Fig 7

3	8	1
2	4	6
7	9	5

Fig 8

2	7	9
1	**3**	5
6	8	4

Fig 9

When you compare the position of number 3 in any of the nine squares with that of the Magic Square (shown below), this gives you the House position that number 3 is occupying in any given square:

- In Fig. 1 number 3 is occupying the 6 House
- In Fig. 2 number 3 is occupying the 7 House
- In Fig. 3 number 3 is occupying the 8 House
- In Fig. 4 number 3 is occupying the 9 House
- In Fig. 5 number 3 is occupying the 1 House

4	9	2
3	5	7
8	1	6

Magic Square

- In Fig. 6 number 3 is occupying the 2 House
- In Fig. 7 number 3 is occupying the 3 House (you will notice that all the numbers here are in their own House)
- In Fig. 8 number 3 is occupying the 4 House
- In Fig. 9 number 3 is at the centre occupying the 5 House

This pattern holds true for both years and months. You are now in a position to determine what House you occupy within any given year. These nine variations of the Magic Square are all you will ever need to understand and use this exciting system of personal navigation.

Overleaf top left is the square that represents 1997 (4 February 1997 to 3 February 1998). Overleaf top right is the Magic Square, which you can now use as a reference point. Superimpose the place where your number appears in the left-hand square on the right-hand square to give you your House position for 1997.

Remember that you can refer to the chart on p. 23 to discover the square for each year.

2	7	9
1	3	5
6	8	4

1997

4	9	2
3	5	7
8	1	6

Magic Square

The Nine Houses

The pattern of the nine Houses is not dissimilar to that of the seasonal growth of plants (see below). You can compare the movement of your own House throughout the nine different squares on pp. 175–6.

4 rapid growth	**9** fame	**2** germination
3 sprouting	**5** fluctuation	**7** celebration
8 stillness	**1** planning	**6** prosperity

Here is a brief outline of the nine Houses:

- *1 Water House (Planning)* In this House your energy is floating deep in the winter, preparing for germination and the spring. It is an excellent time for self-reflection and charting your future.

- *2 Soil House (Germination)* This is a quiet and stagnant House, an excellent time for you to finalise your projects and plans. It is important to remain focused on your projects. Clear out any unwanted baggage in the way of past debts, excess paperwork or clutter in your home.

- *3 Tree House (Sprouting)* This House represents the rising energy of spring and is an excellent House for initiating projects. You can be lucky and energetic, but need to avoid being too impulsive.

- *4 Tree House (Rapid Growth)* This is a continuation of 3 Tree House, with even more capacity for movement and growth. You can tend to get carried away, which can result in your losing stability or momentum. There is an added risk that you could burn out.

- *5 Soil House (Fluctuation)* This is where you enter the House in which you are born. It can be an unpredictable time. You can often feel adolescent, experiencing many new activities and being tempted to move in many different directions. Since you are at the centre, activity and energy are directed at you. Many choices may seem to come your way and it is often difficult to decide what to do. Try to remain centred.

- *6 Metal House (Prosperity)* The previous year's dreams and schemes can begin to bear fruit. In this House you are in the position to harvest what you have been achieving or working towards in the previous few years. You will have good health and stamina but need to maintain some moderation.

- *7 Metal House (Celebration)* After the harvest you can celebrate! This can be a very relaxing House to be in and you can benefit from the prosperity of your endeavour. It is a time for you to relax, to be happy and to reflect on your achievements.

- *8 Soil House (Stillness)* This can be an uncomfortable House for you. There can be times of stillness, and equally sudden or radical change. Since the next House represents the full force of Fire, this House represents the calm before the storm. You can feel uneasy and unsure of what is coming next.

- *9 Fire House (Fame)* Your energy is bright and on the surface for the world to see in this House. You have the greatest opportunity for rapid development and achieving fame. You can be adventurous and optimistic, and your capacity for clear communication can be at its greatest. Try to avoid being stubborn.

Drawing On Your Own Experiences

One of the most effective ways of using this information is to draw from the experiences of your own life. Pick a couple of turning points in your life, for instance a new job, moving house, marriage, separation or an accident, and then discover what year that was in terms of the nine-year cycle. Once you have determined this central number, see what House you were occupying that year. Begin to notice if there was a pattern. (In Chapter 12 we will take a deeper look at these years, right down to individual months.)

Another useful way of understanding this subject is to look at your current relationships. To do this you check what House you are occupying this year relative to those of the people in question. It can shed light on a different perspective within a relationship. For example, you may be occupying the 3 House this year. This could lead you to being impulsive, outgoing, excited and enthusiastic for travel, change or exploration. On the other hand, your partner may be in the 1 Water House. He or she would not be so keen to socialise or travel, preferring to stay at home on a Saturday night rather than to party, and while you might be keen to go scuba-diving in the Caribbean they might prefer to go walking in the English countryside. You may also wish to look at the relationship between yourself and your colleagues at work. Why are some getting recognition? Why is an individual suddenly coming up with innovative ideas? Why is someone else who is normally outgoing and flamboyant appearing changeable and indecisive this year?

It is this kind of research over the last 18 years that has brought this subject alive for me. We have all had ups and downs in our lives, and 9 Star Ki astrology can show these events from a new and exciting perspective. I hope that the anecdotes and experiences that I shall share as we go through the nine Houses in more detail will help you to discover new approaches to your future.

1 Water House (Planning)

Symbolism

This House occupies the north in the Magic Square. Facing away from the sun, this space represents night and winter. When you occupy this House you too will feel withdrawn, quiet and contemplative. As in the natural world, the energy is still. You do not see squirrels running around in midwinter, nor do you see leaves appearing on trees. However, this does not mean that nature is dead: there is plenty of activity occurring beneath the surface in preparation for the re-emergence of spring.

Interpretation

When you occupy this House you may feel that you have been left out and that your dreams and schemes are on the back burner. Because your natural energy at this time is introverted, you may experience difficulties communicating with friends and the outside world. Similarly, your energy will appear to others to be more withdrawn, so communication from them will be equally reticent. This can be a somewhat vulnerable time – in the same way as when you are asleep – and you need to make an extra effort to protect yourself. This vulnerability can be associated with: being misunderstood, with health problems, with financial problems or with being robbed.

The winter mode in which you find yourself in the 1 Water House can make you very intuitive and hypersensitive, which can lead you to make unnecessary or rash decisions based on a false experience of a situation. It is wise, therefore, to guard against making such decisions based on fear. At the same time, listen very carefully to what other people are saying so that you do not misunderstand them. In the same way you should be very clear in your communication with others and very grounded in your actions.

You will find that your intuitive nature will be at its strongest in the 1 Water House. This is a perfect time for you to see the big picture, which will enable you to chart your future.

Recommendations

Most of us who live in a four-seasons climate draw little inspiration from the winter. However, it is a valuable part of the cycle. In nature it enables new growth to develop under the surface, while it gives human beings a chance to reflect on the previous year and make plans for the following one. In the same way it is wise to remain calm and be patient.

This is a perfect opportunity to reflect on the previous few years and to begin to plan the next stage of the cycle.

During this time try to be adaptable to situations. This is an excellent House to occupy in terms of developing the spiritual side of your nature. To take up meditation, T'ai Chi Chuan, yoga and so on during this time is very auspicious. If you are interested in the concept of oriental philosophy, this would be an ideal time to study or practise the use of the *I Ching*.

Try to avoid launching new undertakings this year – it is not the most auspicious time. You may find that misunderstandings, miscommunications and small trying obstacles get in your way. This year will be far better spent in carefully planning your future.

Health

The Water element in Chinese medicine controls the health and function of the kidneys, the bladder and the reproductive system. During this time these organs are more likely to recharge themselves or to display symptoms of any underlying problems. Health problems associated with fluid could also arise. These could relate to living somewhere damp or excessively cold, to consuming too much in general or to drinking too much alcohol. Try to reduce your intake of food and drink that is excessively cold – taken directly from the fridge without being allowed to heat up to at least room temperature.

Since this is a somewhat stagnant House, past problems with your general health tend to reappear. Contemplating and planning for the future is auspicious during this year.

Considerations for the nine principal numbers

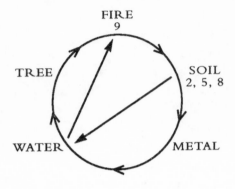

If you are a 9 Fire or a 2, 5 or 8 Soil, you may experience more unease and discomfort when you occupy this House.

Examples

The French philosopher Jean-Paul Sartre (5 Soil), was occupying the number 1 Water House when in 1964 he refused the Nobel Prize for Literature.

8	4	6
7	9	2
3	5	1

In World War I heroine nurse Edith Cavell (9 Fire) helped British and Allied soldiers escape from the Netherlands. She was arrested and tried by the Germans, sentenced to death and shot three days later. At the time she was occupying the 1 Water House, which can make us more vulnerable but at the same time gives us the greatest opportunity to see the overall picture. On the eve of her execution she wrote, 'Standing, as I do, in view of God and eternity, I realise that patriotism is not enough. I must have no hatred or bitterness towards anyone.'

3	8	1
2	4	6
7	**9**	5

2 Soil House (Germination)

Symbolism

In this House you occupy the south-west position, which is where the sun has just left midday or midsummer. It is that quiet period between noon and 3 p.m. when the atmospheric conditions can appear unmoving. In hot climates this is a favourite time for siesta. In terms of season, it is the late summer when the harvest is in and farmers are preparing for the next stage, which could be ploughing the fields before sowing.

Interpretation

When you occupy this House you retain some of the stagnation from the previous year (1 Water House): your natural energy is still in the process of slowing down and you will appear and feel inactive. It is quite normal to feel isolated and perhaps lonely during this year. Socially and financially it is a time of slow or little growth.

This House is the perfect space in which to get all the areas of your life in order before your re-emergence in the 3 House in the following year. Take care of all the small details, which will slow you down if they are not clearly defined now.

Recommendations

Because your own natural energy tends to be stagnant during this House, try not to lead or take initiative for new action during this year. It is wise to maintain some self-control despite your excitement about future plans. Your energy is in a perfect position to listen, to observe and to share your dreams and schemes with others.

It is good to continue formulating your plans for the future during this year. Make a list of what you need to set up for initiating some new project, which could be a change of job, relationship or home. You are in a good position to raise small loans, perhaps a deposit on a house. Consider what other forms of support you might need for your plans: have preliminary conversations with partners in an enterprise, for example. Because your energy is naturally quieter this year, try to appear modest and be sincere in all your conversations and undertakings.

For real success in any venture you need to clear up any outstanding commitments that might impede your progress. This 'weeding' process, combined with careful, modest planning and a sincere expression of your desires and dreams, will make your future ventures far more successful.

Health

The element Soil in Chinese medicine represents the functions of the stomach, the pancreas and the spleen. Associated with these organs is the wellbeing of your lymphatic system. If we do not take enough exercise our circulation and lymphatic system can stagnate. The latter system can be stimulated by rubbing your skin morning and evening with a hot, damp towel and by keeping yourself physically active. When we occupy the 2 House we are in a more still position than usual, and it is important to balance this with physical activity that fills our lungs and bloodstream with oxygen and makes us sweat.

Emotionally, the Soil element can express itself negatively through worry, anxiety, suspicion, cynicism and complaint. Try to guard against letting these emotions cloud your judgement or get in the way of your future dreams.

Considerations for the nine principal numbers

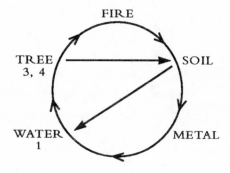

If you are 1 Water, 3 Tree or 4 Tree when you occupy the 2 House, you may find it more challenging than the other numbers.

Examples

The American gangster Al Capone (3 Tree) was finally arrested, tried and imprisoned by the US Government in 1931 when he was occupying the 2 House.

5	1	**3**
4	6	8
9	2	7

Queen Victoria (1 Water) began her retreat from public life in 1861 when her husband Prince Albert (1 Water) died. She was occupying the 2 House.

3	8	**1**
2	4	6
7	9	5

3 Tree House (Sprouting)

Symbolism

The House represents east in the Magic Square and therefore the nature of dawn. Sunrise is symbolic of new growth and new development. East can also symbolise the emergence of spring with all its accompanying rising energy. The trigram from the *I Ching* is Chen – arousing Thunder. It represents the full force of initiating new changes, a new dawn and new opportunities.

Interpretation

When you occupy this House the previous two years (1 Water and 2 Soil) begin to fade into the background. Those years represent the planning stages, and now you can start putting those plans into action. The stagnation of the previous two years will lift and you will feel enthusiastic, confident and impulsive.

Because progress will be rapid when you occupy this House, it is important to ensure that you are on course towards your dreams. In the same way that progress can be rapid, so can success or failure. It is all down to your personal navigation and your ability to take care of details along the way. Because you are moving so fast during this year it is important to remain focused.

When you occupy this House your creativity is at its strongest and your ideas can flow effortlessly. Your expression and talents all have the potential to shine through very strongly.

Recommendations

This is the perfect year to start a new adventure and you are in an excellent position to take advantage of the new energy of dawn and spring. This could be an excellent time for you to travel. Having the full force of spring behind you can bring you tremendous luck, and you would be wise not to brag about this to others: others who are not occupying the 3 House may be secretly jealous of your successes.

While being driven along by this new-found enthusiastic energy, take care not to overlook important details. Small mistakes can hinder your progress.

This House will bring you great opportunity for change and new developments. Try to be flexible in accommodating new ideas and new perspectives. It would also be wise to go with this new energy rather than being hesitant. In a future House you may regret having procrastinated about initiating a new project.

Because this House is one of the most active (yang) spaces that you occupy in the Magic Square, try to balance this with some yin recreation. Make the effort to slow down, relax and recharge your batteries. When you are on a roll it is hard to contemplate slowing down, but make the effort to book an aromatherapy massage or have a sauna or a lazy Sunday off. And let your newly discovered dynamism rub off on to those around you – your enthusiasm can be an inspiration to others at this time.

Health

Because your natural energy this year can be impulsive and impetuous, you should take special care to avoid accidents. Undue carelessness can cause you unnecessary cuts and bruises.

In Chinese medicine Tree energy governs the functions of the liver and gall bladder. The best support that you can give these systems is to avoid eating late at night (less than two hours before going to bed), over-eating and eating too large a breakfast before undertaking any physical activity.

The emotionally negative aspect of any imbalance in the liver and gall bladder can be expressed as anger. Since this year you are in a space of advancement and movement, you may feel unusually frustrated or angry if you are held back.

Considerations for the nine principal numbers

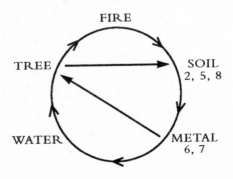

If you are a 2, 5 or 8 Soil or a 6 or 7 Metal, pay particular attention to detail this year and avoid being too impetuous.

Examples

In 1953, Sir Edmund Hillary (9 Fire) successfully conquered Mount Everest while occupying the 3 House.

1	6	8
9	2	4
5	7	3

The Russian dictator Josef Stalin (4 Tree) returned from exile after the Russian Revolution and became General Secretary of the Communist Party in 1922. Although there was a power struggle between Stalin, Lenin and Trotsky, at this time Stalin was occupying a prestigious position (3 House).

5	1	3
4	6	8
9	2	7

4 Tree House (Rapid Growth)

Symbolism

The number 4 House is in the south-east corner of the
Magic Square, which represents mid-morning or late
spring. This is symbolic of a continuation of the previous
house (3 Tree) and its upward growth. The trigram from
the *I Ching* is Sun, which means Wind and can be interpreted as changeable and potentially unstable – movement
without stability. You will notice that the bottom line of the
trigram is broken (yin), giving little stability to the upper
two yang lines.

Interpretation

This is the year when the planning stages of the 1 and 2
House, in combination with the initiating qualities of the 3
House, begin to bear fruit in the 4 House. Carefully
thought out plans and well-implemented initiatives can
now start to bear fruit. This is where your past can catch up
with you – whether favourable or unfavourable.

Since you will be riding on the energy of this light
upward movement of Tree, you will appear bright,
expressive and happy. When you appear optimistic your
opportunities for advancement are greater. This potential
advancement is excellent, provided that it is structured.
Your communication with others is particularly good, and
what you have to say is respected and trusted. This is a
very good House from which to obtain credit or a loan
based on your current situation and your previous detailed
plans.

Recommendations

It is important to remember the concept of movement
without stability. Despite your optimistic state of mind,

reserve some energy for caution because this is not a good time to be impetuous. It is very tempting when you occupy this House to change direction or move away from what you have been planning and initiating in the previous few years, but this is not a good move. The best advice is to follow through on the successes of the previous year. Continue growing and developing whatever you planned in your 1 and 2 House – after all, in mid-spring a farmer would not decide to pull up all his flourishing crops and start growing something completely different.

This lack of stability can endanger you if you decide to take up a new venture with which you are not completely familiar. Try to stay with what you know best, and develop it. Since you feel a sense of unbridled enthusiasm, try not to make rash promises: keep your word and follow through on any commitments that you make.

Health

Taking into account the symbolism of the trigram Sun, you must take care not to burn yourself out. Since this trigram lacks stability at its base you may find yourself rushing in too many directions, using your intellect and nervous system and at the same time not grounding yourself. To avoid exhaustion follow a fairly rigorous exercise programme that keeps you grounded. You may also tend to forget details and to appear scatty. Remember that the 4 Tree House is connected with the function of the liver in Chinese medicine, so be wary not to suppress any frustration or anger.

Considerations for the other nine principal numbers

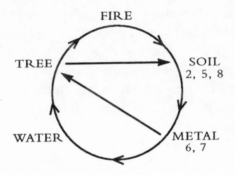

If you are a 2, 5, or 8 Soil or a 6 or 7 Metal, be particularly careful when you occupy this House.

Examples

Judge Jeffreys (4 Tree), was notorious for his merciless treatment of the supporters of a rebellion during the reign of James II. When James left England Jeffreys was captured and in 1689 he died in the Tower of London while occupying the 4 House.

4	9	2
3	5	7
8	1	6

Nicolae Ceaucescu (1 Water), the Romanian dictator, was deposed in December 1989. He and his wife were executed on Christmas Day that year, when he was occupying the 4 House.

1	6	8
9	2	4
5	7	3

5 Soil House (Fluctuation)

Symbolism

We are all born into this House and return there at the age of nine, 18, 27, 36, 45, 54 and so on. Being at the centre of this system is symbolic of the beginning and end of the cycle. This is associated with the peak of accomplishment based on what you have been striving for in recent years.

Interpretation

This can be a very unpredictable House to occupy. You are at the end of one cycle and about to begin a new phase. Since the stars are now symbolically positioned just as they were the year of your birth, you can go through an experience of renewing yourself.

When you are at the centre, all the other numbers are focused in your direction. People will naturally gravitate towards you, seeking your advice and threatening to deplete you of time and energy. Many new opportunities will show themselves during this year, and it may be hard to choose which direction to take.

This is also a House of extremes. Whatever you have been striving for in recent years has every opportunity to come to fruition – what you have sown you will reap – you may be rewarded for your efforts or penalised for your poor judgement.

New ventures that are initiated when you occupy the 5 House can have a long-lasting effect and need to be considered very carefully. However, many people find this an excellent year for making changes in a relationship or discovering a new love.

Recommendations

Since you will feel pulled in many directions this year, it is good advice to keep still. Try not to be frenetic in your actions, and be modest in your indulgences. While many people will gravitate towards you, try to keep centred and develop your sense of compassion for them without letting yourself feel drained.

This is an excellent year in which to pause and reflect. Aim to avoid making long journeys or moving home. It is your year to find yourself and to express your real potential to others around you. Only make moves or initiate new projects if you are really convinced of their likely success.

Health

Pay particular attention to your emotional wellbeing when you occupy this House because so many demands may be made on you and you will be drawn in many different directions. Avoid extremes in your lifestyle, diet and exercise programme.

In this House, there is potential for health problems to recur if they have not been properly addressed during the previous nine years. This is especially true of problems that first emerged nine or 18 years earlier when you previously occupied the number 5 House.

Considerations for the nine principal numbers

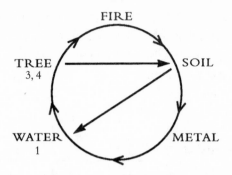

If you are a 3 or 4 Tree or 1 Water, pay particular attention to the advice given above when you are occupying the 5 House.

Examples

Nelson Mandela (1 Water), who since 1964 had been imprisoned in South Africa as a banned member of the African National Congress, was finally released after a tireless international campaign in 1990. He was occupying the 5 House.

9	5	7
8	**1**	3
4	6	2

The British poet and adventurer Lord Byron (5 Soil) described his own character in a way that was quite consistent with a 5 Soil nature: 'I am so changeable ... such a

strange mélange of good and evil. . . . There are two senti-
ments to which I am constant – a strong love of liberty and
a detestation of cant, and neither is calculated to gain me
friends.' He travelled to Greece, but the long journey and
poor conditions gave him a fever and he died in 1824 while
occupying the 5 House.

4	9	2
3	5	7
8	1	6

6 Metal House (Prosperity)

Symbolism

In this House you occupy the north-west, symbolic of late
autumn or evening. This House represents the fulfilment of
your previous year's endeavours – a chance to harvest. The
trigram from the *I Ching* is Ch'ien, and it gives you the full
force and authority of the yang symbolism of heaven.

Interpretation

This is an excellent House to occupy as you begin to reap
the rewards of your previous year's efforts. It is quite likely
that your skills and talents will be noticed by others, which
could lead, for instance, to a pay rise, more responsibility or
a better job.

This is a good year to travel. Your abilities will be noticed and you will feel confident and right most of the time. It is a good year to fulfil your ambitions. The presence of heaven in your chart brings clarity, focus and leadership to you when you occupy this space.

Recommendations

Keep your goals clearly in mind. Work towards fulfilling your ambitions, but do not walk over others. Be careful not to show off your new-found confidence to others who perhaps lack it at present, or you could create enmity. Try not to come across as self-righteous.

The autumn is symbolic of gathering in, so despite your tremendous enthusiasm try to be frugal and if possible avoid lending and borrowing. Despite your confidence, heed the advice of others around you.

Health

Look after yourself during this time, primarily by taking plenty of rest – do not exhaust yourself, as it could take you some time to recover. When we become tired or ill in the late autumn it frequently takes us much longer to recuperate than when we are ill in the spring or summer. Keep yourself flexible, as you have a tendency to become more yang (tight) when occupying this House and can become physically and mentally more rigid.

Take care of your bones – ensure that you have sufficient minerals and vitamin D in your diet. Take care when travelling to avoid accidents.

Considerations for the nine principal numbers

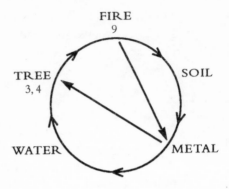

If you are a 3 or 4 Tree or a 9 Fire pay special attention to the advice above when you occupy the 6 House.

Examples

Henry Tudor, the Lancastrian claimant to the English throne, defeated and killed the Yorkist King Richard III at the Battle of Bosworth and became King Henry VII. Henry was in his 6 House. During his reign he broke the power of the English nobility, and the wealth that he took from them was inherited by his son Henry VIII.

1	6	8
9	2	4
5	7	3

Robert the Bruce (6 Metal) led the Scots against the English in battle. After his success, in 1328 Scotland became independent and Robert was declared King. He was occupying the 6 House.

4	9	2
3	5	7
8	1	6

7 Metal House (Celebration)

Symbolism

Here you occupy the west in the Magic Square, representing the sunset. Seasonally this is autumn – a chance to reflect and to celebrate your past efforts. The symbolism from the trigram Tui is Joy. This House represents entertainment, relaxation and reflection.

Interpretation

Of all the nine Houses, this one offers you the path of least resistance. Generally, things will go smoothly. You can feel relaxed and confident: this is a time to socialise more and broaden your horizons.

The concept of 'harvest' today could mean that you received a pay rise, or you might 'harvest' money from an unexpected source such as the lottery or an inheritance. But there is an equal chance that you may spend more, partly due to your more relaxed lifestyle and your desire to socialise and to eat out more frequently.

You need to be cautious in your communications with others. Misunderstandings can arise regarding details of agreements, or about what you have said or claimed.

Recommendations

Occupying the 7 Metal House gives you a unique opportunity to experience two quite different aspects of your life, relaxation and reflection. You now have the perfect opportunity to put your feet up or let your hair down! You may be drawn to a busy social life, or you may feel released from any burden of responsibility that you bore in the preceding six years and have a deeper sense of relaxation and fulfilment. Traditionally, this is the time of celebration after the harvest: family, friends and neighbours would gather to eat and drink and feast and dance. In the same way that a traditional farmer might sit at sunset on his porch watching the sun going down over the land, pause to reflect. A good farmer will consider what he has learnt from today and what he can bring to his tasks tomorrow.

But occupying the 7 House is not all party time, and the results of overdoing things are inevitable. This is a perfect time to review your own deeper mental and spiritual state. Long country walks on your own can be very beneficial. Next year you will enter the 8 House, and the more reflective preparation you have had now in the 7 House the better you will be able to ride through the following year.

Where relationships are concerned, you tend to feel more attracted to others when you occupy the 7 House. Unfortunately, most of your encounters are superficial and therefore disappointing and short-lived.

Health

This is generally a good year for you. The symbolism for Joy brings energy and stamina. Take care not to suffer needless accidents, especially to your bones.

Traditional Chinese medicine sees the element Metal as controlling the function of the lungs and large intestine. Autumn is the time of year associated with these organs. If either becomes weak or neglected it can lead to a feeling of depression, isolation and sadness.

Considerations for the other nine numbers

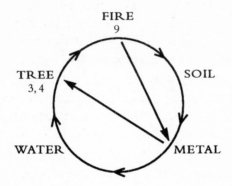

If you are a 3 or 4 Tree or a 9 Fire, pay particular attention to the warnings above.

Examples

From the 1920s Mao Tse-tung (8 Soil) waged a long struggle with first the Chinese warlords and later the Nationalists. In 1949 be became the first chairman of the People's Republic of China when he was occupying the 7 House.

5	1	3
4	6	**8**
9	2	7

The dramatist Christopher Marlowe (4 Tree) was killed in a London tavern brawl in 1593 while occupying the 7 House. At the time he was under suspicion by the authorities for having written subversive pamphlets. His death and its suspicious circumstances remain a mystery to this day.

1	6	8
9	2	**4**
5	7	3

8 Soil House (Stillness)

Symbolism

This House occupies the north-east position of the Magic Square, which represents the transition from winter to spring or the time between midnight and dawn. Essentially this is the calm before the storm – the storm will come when you enter the 9 House in the next year.

Interpretation

The trigram Ken from the *I Ching* is translated as the Mountain, and evokes an image of stillness. For the most part this can be a stagnant year in which it is very easy for you to retreat into your 'cave' deep within the Mountain. You can easily be misunderstood and you need to express yourself more clearly than usual. Remember that communication goes both ways – you need to listen carefully as well.

Change is definitely in the air. Decisions about change can be brought about by either external pressure or internal reflection.

Recommendations

Your quietness and stillness this year may upset others if you retreat and become stubborn. Try not to be rigid or push your ideas too hard, as this will cause antagonism. Aim to be sincere in whatever you undertake, and give yourself plenty of time. It is fine to be slow and even ponderous in taking action.

Big changes in your life can work well this year, provided they are generally in line with your dream. A total reversal of direction or undertaking a completely new venture with which you are not familiar is not wise.

Generally, try to keep calm and be very aware of what is going on around you. If you find yourself retreating into your 'cave' force yourself out and keep on top of developments at work, at home and in the world. Try to restrain any rebellious spirit that you have during this year, as it is most likely to be misunderstood and to cause unnecessary antagonism towards you.

Health

Since this is a stagnant year you should keep yourself as active as possible. Keep an eye out for problems with your circulation and lymphatic system, which crop up when we do not take enough exercise.

Be careful of arguments that could lead to fights, with you coming out on the losing side. You can also be more vulnerable this year, so take care to avoid accidents in particular when caused by others.

Considerations for the other nine numbers

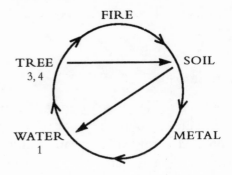

If your principal number is 1 Water or 3 or 4 Tree be especially careful to avoid stagnation. The quietness and stillness of this House may bring a bigger desire for change for you in particular.

Examples

O.J. Simpson (8 Soil) retreated into the 'cave' within his Mountain during his trial in 1995 and refused to give testimony. However, that was the calm before the storm, because in 1996 he faced a further trial while occupying the 9 House.

3	8	1
2	4	6
7	9	5

The Argentinian revolutionary Che Guevara (9 Fire) fought successfully alongside Fidel Castro in Cuba but was later captured and shot by the Bolivian Army while he was occupying the 8 House.

5	1	3
4	6	8
9	2	7

9 Fire House (Fame)

Symbolism

In this House you occupy the south position in the Magic Square which, according to the Chinese maps, is facing the heat, the sun and the south. This House is symbolic of mid-day and midsummer and brings brightness, fame and clarity.

Interpretation

When you occupy this House you have the greatest potential to fulfil your ambitions and dreams. Whatever you have been working towards in the previous years has great potential to be realised.

Fire is illuminating and revealing by nature. In this House your past becomes known. If you are striving to have, say, your invention or your status recognised, this is your chance. Equally, if you have been hiding some aspect of your life it is more likely to be revealed now: an affair may become public knowledge, or your tax affairs may come under closer scrutiny. Your natural energy is brighter and you are more easily noticed when you are in this House.

It is easy for you to make new friends at this time, but equally easy to lose some old friends. An analogy would be going on holiday to a warm climate with old friends. You might find that the heat and the activity does not suit the relationship that you had in a cooler climate. Yet in the heat you might find new friends who suit your nature at the time.

Recommendations

All fire needs a firm foundation for it to remain useful, functional and warming. So make an effort to build a firm base for any ideas or projects that you set in motion this particular year.

This is a year in which you value your independence and freedom. Fire's nature is expansive and expressive, which can be translated as your desire to seek variety in lifestyle, in recreation and new ventures. Others around you may not be of the same mind as they may be occupying different Houses at this time, so in your relationships with others be very open and frank about what you are looking for.

Above all, be positive. This is essentially a bright and enjoyable House, when the efforts of the past years can be recognised and your talents and energy will be noticed. Make use of it.

Health

Remember that fire burns with fuel, which in this instance means you! Take extra care of your health so that you do not burn out. 'Fire' in traditional Chinese medicine controls the function of the heart and small intestine. If you are prone to high blood pressure or heart disease, be especially careful this year. You are also more prone to fevers at this time. Be very cautious near fire so as to avoid burns and scalds.

Considerations for the other nine numbers

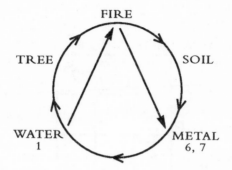

If you are a 1 Water or a 6 or 7 Metal you may feel the fire more while you occupy this House. It may cause you some discomfort and you need to be especially careful with your health, particularly the circulatory system.

Examples

The Argentinian soccer player Diego Maradonna (4 Tree) was admired worldwide for his incredible skills. In 1991, while occupying the 9 House, he was banned from world-class football for 18 months when it was discovered that he was using cocaine.

8	4	6
7	9	2
3	5	1

James VI of Scotland (5 Soil) acceded to the throne in 1567 on the abdication of his mother, Mary Queen of Scots. Then, on the death of his mother's half-sister Elizabeth I in 1603, he also became King James I of England, uniting the thrones of England and Scotland. He was occupying the 9 House.

9	5	7
8	1	3
4	6	2

12

MONTHLY PREDICTIONS

In the previous chapter you will have discovered the flavour of what is in store for you within any of the nine years (Houses). The months can be treated as a similar nine-part sequence in which the progression of the Houses is identical to that of the years – that is, they move from 9 through to 1 and then begin again at 9.

The effect on you of the month is more immediate than that of the year and tends to affect your emotions more. For example, if in a year in which you were occupying the 6 House, a relatively stable (yang) House, you found yourself in the 3 House in a particular month, you would be likely to feel spontaneous, outgoing and impulsive. In other words, the experience for the month can over-ride the flavour for the year – and you can use this feature to your advantage. If, for instance, you were in a 1 Water House for the year (which leaves you on the back burner while you contemplate and chart your future), rather than completely write off that year you could select one of the more active months for taking a holiday or initiating some change at work.

How to Work Out the Monthly Predictions

Which House do you occupy in any given year?

Chapter 11 will show you what House you occupy in any given year (running, as usual, from 4 February to 3 February). This gives you the overall energy that you will be experiencing for that particular year. Decide which number (1–9) represents the 'year' of the month that you wish to look at. Look for the 'year' in one of the three right-hand columns below.

What kind of month do you occupy?

Find the relevant date in the left-hand column of the chart. Now move across to whichever column contains the number of your House for the year in question. The number opposite the date is the one you want.

Birth Date	1, 4, 7	5, 2, 8	3, 6, 9
4 February to 5 March	8	2	5
6 March to 5 April	7	1	4
6 April to 5 May	6	9	3
6 May to 5 June	5	8	2
6 June to 7 July	4	7	1
8 July to 7 August	3	6	9
8 August to 7 September	2	5	8
8 September to 8 October	1	4	7
9 October to 7 November	9	3	6
8 November to 7 December	8	2	5
8 December to 5 January	7	1	4
6 January to 3 February	6	9	3

Example

Let us say that the date you are interested in is 13 August 1982. Since 1982 was a 9 Fire year, you look for the number 9 in one of the right-hand column headings. Now drop down that column until you are opposite '8 August to 7 September' in the left-hand column. The presence of the figure 8 tells you that 13 August 1982 occurred in an 8 month.

The nine-month Houses

Set out overleaf is the progression of the nine-month Houses, moving from 9 to 1. It can be used for any months, past or future.

The Experience of Each Month

Here is a summary of how you may feel in any given House that you occupy in any month. Remember that you need to combine this with the overall flavour of the yearly House that you occupy. In addition, you could interpret what your principal number would feel occupying the year and the House. The possibilities are enormous.

1 Water House

In this House you can feel introverted, quiet and perhaps vulnerable. Communication with others is harder than usual and you may feel left out. It is a month in which you are more likely to reflect deeply and be attracted to spiritual practices such as meditation.

8	4	6
7	9	2
3	5	1

7	3	5
6	8	1
2	4	9

6	2	4
5	7	9
1	3	8

5	1	3
4	6	8
9	2	7

4	9	2
3	5	7
8	1	6

3	8	1
2	4	6
7	9	5

2	7	9
1	3	5
6	8	4

1	6	8
9	2	4
5	7	3

9	5	7
8	1	3
4	6	2

2 Soil House

While occupying this House you will feel stillness and stagnation. However, you may experience the urge to become more active, and may feel disappointed if you make the effort to socialise or air your ideas but are still ignored. This is an excellent month for formulating plans and ideas.

3 Tree House

You feel lucky and enthusiastic in this House. You have potential for enormous energy, drive and spontaneity.

4 Tree House

Generally this is a happy and productive House to occupy. You feel positive, and if you are not careful you can get carried away with your ideas and enthusiasm. Try to pace yourself to avoid burning out.

5 Soil House

Aim to remain still and centred this month. You will feel like an adolescent: with plenty of opportunities coming your way, and new experiences to try, you are often not sure which way to go. It can be an unpredictable and emotional month with big ups and big downs.

6 Metal House

During this month you feel clear, strong and purposeful. Be wary not to impose your will on others. You feel so positive and right about what you are doing that you risk becoming inflexible, which could upset people around you.

7 Metal House

This House gives you the opportunity to have fun and be active. You may feel carefree and adventurous. If in previous months you have been reticent about socialising, now is the time to break out. Conversely, spend some of the time reflecting and preparing yourself for the 8 House.

8 Soil House

In this House you may feel unsure about your future. You are quieter than usual and need time to retreat into yourself. Try to avoid impulsive action, and talk through your worries and fears with a close friend.

9 Fire House

If it is a relatively quieter year for you (1, 2 or 8 House), this is the month to see a break in that pattern. Your energy can be enthusiastic, adventurous and fun. But remember that those around you may not be occupying the same House and may not wish to be so active. If your communication with others has been poor in recent months, now is the time to make yourself clear.

Examples

Before the Spanish Grand Prix of 2 June 1996 (a 4 Tree year/5 month) Damon Hill (4 Tree) was in pole position. (Remember that although this date is in June you need to look at the square for May, as June does not 'begin' until the 6th.) On the morning of the race he asked his mechanics for even more power. In May that year he was occupying the 4 House – movement without stability. In the wet conditions he spun off the track and lost the race. The Japanese Grand Prix of October 1996 would decide the new World Champion. This time Damon Hill was occupying the 9 Fire

House, which gave him maximum opportunity for fame – either great success or great failure. In the event he won. In the same race, however, Eddie Irvine (8 Soil) was occupying the 4 House, movement without stability (see below). He shunted two cars and eventually spun off himself.

8	4	6
7	9	2
3	5	1

13

TRAVEL PLANS

Directionology is another fascinating aspect of 9 House astrology. It can be used to determine the best direction in which to move house or relocate your office. Major moves are really based on the House that you occupy within any given year of your move. However, for short-term travel plans you can refer to the month in question provided the journey takes less than one month.

As discussed in Chapter 3, this body of knowledge that we call 9 House astrology comes from an understanding of the *I Ching*, which may be five thousand years old. In the past people regarded travel or moving home as a major event in their lives and would have followed their intuition and astrological predictions to make the best of the situation. Even in early twentieth-century Britain many children from the industrial cities never saw the sea.

Nowadays we think little of such events, but moves into a city or out to the country do have an effect on our body's chi. For example, it is a yangising experience to move to the city and generally more yinising to move to the country. In the same way moving to the mountains can be yangising, whereas a move to a warmer coastal region can be yinising. Many Americans choose to retire to Florida, where the chi energy is governed by the humidity. When I went there I felt lethargic, slow and unenthusiastic. In many ways it is a natural attraction to want to spend your remaining years in a natural environment that is slowly 'sinking'.

If you use 9 Star Ki to assist you in your move, you will understand where your natural energy is flowing at the moment and what would best support you. The examples of directions in this chapter, together with their strengths and weaknesses, can really help you optimise your plans.

The Magic Square

Your compass for this form of directionology is the basic Magic Square and the eight other versions of it. Remember that the south and the sun (Fire position) are at the top, since in the traditional Chinese view of the world the sun was in the south. Familiarise yourself with this unconventional north/south/east/west arrangement to avoid making any mistakes in your calculations.

	SOUTH	
4	9	2
3	5	7
8	1	6

S E (top left)   S W (top right)
EAST (left middle)   WEST (right middle)
N E (bottom left)   N W (bottom right)
NORTH (bottom)

When looking at any particular time for intended travel, begin by drawing the square of the year or month involved. Highlight the space that you occupy and the one that the number 5 occupies, within the relevant square. This is a good reference point for determining whether any of the Six Inauspicious Directions (see below) are present within your chart. If all is clear, then the move looks good.

Remember that all directions you undertake pass through the centre.

The Six Inauspicious Directions

Avoid travelling towards your own number

For the purpose of understanding and studying this system of directionology, imagine that you are a 9 Fire person. When you look at the square below which has 2 at the centre (indicating that it is either a 2 year or a 2 month) you will notice that the 9 is occupying the position east. Since you must avoid travelling towards your own number, in this particular instance the interpretation is not to move east.

1	6	8
9	2	4
5	7	3

EAST (left)   WEST (right)

If you move towards your own number, what might happen? Your energy is likely to become internalised because you are moving towards yourself, and as a result you could become isolated, introverted or withdrawn. For instance, if in the example above you were planning a holiday which involved travelling east and you intended to have a good time, you should not be surprised if you ended up staying in your hotel room reading a book and taking very little interest in what is going on around you. Similarly, if you decided nevertheless to undertake a major move from which you hoped to gain more recognition for your work, you might well find yourself being left out and having trouble communicating with the outside world. If you have made a move like this, the easiest solution is to make more of an effort to let people know where you are and what you are doing. Do not assume that you will come to people's attention easily – you need to make more effort than usual to communicate with others.

Avoid travelling away from your number

In this instance, if you refer to the chart the direction is west.

1	6	8
9	2	**4**
5	7	3

EAST (left) · WEST (right)

Moving away from your number is the same as moving away from yourself. The interpretation is that you will feel off your guard, vulnerable and open to making mistakes. You are losing your centre. You are likely to be forgetful, to lose track of time and even to lose your sense of purpose or direction.

If you have planned a holiday in this direction for several months, with clear intentions of what you want to achieve, it may not turn out that way. You may end up going with the flow or just tagging along with what everyone else wants to do. At times you may feel out of your depth, leading to feelings of frustration and perhaps isolation.

If you do make a journey like this, keep practising some kind of discipline that keeps you centred – say yoga, meditation or Chi-Kung. Take time to review what you want to do, and make more effort than usual to keep focused.

Avoid travelling towards number 5

In this system of directionology the number 5 House is always symbolic of potential obvious danger. In this instance it would be a move in a north-eastern direction.

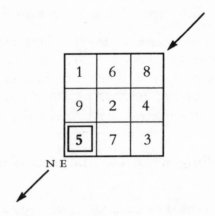

Obvious danger is interpreted as those predictable elements in your journey or holiday that you already knew could cause trouble. For example, if you are a 9 Fire moving house in a north-easterly direction and your surveyor's report reveals that you have some woodworm in the floorboards, take particular care. Do not assume that the problem does not really exist.

Avoid travelling away from 5

This kind of move symbolises potential danger from the unexpected. There is very little that you can do to offset the risk except to be always on your guard, centred and ready for anything.

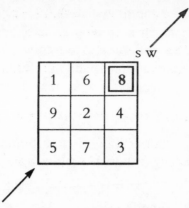

In the square the wrong move would be one in the south-west direction. So if you are taking a short holiday in the south-west pay particular attention to all aspects of your journey and the planning of it. Allow more time than usual for your trip to the airport, and allow time for delays at all stages. Take particular care of your travel documents and money.

Avoid travelling when your number is in the centre

In this case your number is occupying the central House (5). When you are at the centre you are gathering in energy from all directions and your focus needs to be on yourself, in particular reflecting on the past and planning the future.

8	4	6
7	9	2
3	5	1

It is not a wise time to travel or make major moves. If, however, you must, be very careful. The journey could be chaotic, and you may cause confusion to others as well as creating misunderstandings for yourself. When you occupy the centre, try to remain grounded in all senses.

Avoid travelling when number 5 is in the centre

When the number 5 is at the centre, all the principal numbers are in their own House.

4	9	2
3	5	7
8	1	6

This is a time when all the nine Houses have an opportunity to replenish and recharge themselves. A move, especially one that is long-term, is particularly inauspicious at this time. It can be destabilising and disorientating. When 5 is at the centre and all the numbers are in their own Houses, use the time wisely to regather and regroup your nature.

Examples

Lord Mountbatten (1 Water) was murdered in August 1979 by IRA terrorists who blew up his boat in the west of Ireland. August was a 5 month.

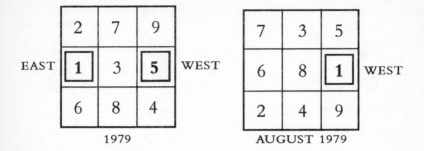

As you can see from the square above left, 1979 was a 3 year; 1 Water occupied the east and 5 occupied the west. This represented a double danger, as Mountbatten's principal number was also opposite 5. The square above right represents August 1979, when 1 Water occupied the position west – the position of vulnerability.

Getting the Best Out of Travel

Now that you are familiar with this system of directionology it would be a good idea to make a list of journeys that you have made that went well or badly. Use the system described in this chapter to see if there is any correlation with the House that you occupied, the position of 5 and the nature of the journey that you undertook. But remember that although this system is based on numbers, at the end of the day all travel and all direction is based on your own intuition. Learn to listen to your own misgivings before you make a journey, and do not act purely in regard to time constraints, economic factors or even directionology.

Useful Tips

Try to adjust yourself some days in advance of the journey that you are about to undertake. For example, if you are planning to take a tropical holiday in winter, get into the mood a few days before you leave. Relax and imagine yourself basking in the sun. Begin to slow down. Perhaps begin to eat and drink the kinds of food that will be available when you arrive. All of this helps to tune you in on an energetic level to your destination. What you should not do is rush around madly, dash to the airport, and then arrive stressed and disorientated.

If, when you plan a journey, you discover that you are not particularly well placed in terms of direction, do not necessarily abandon it. Check out the Houses that your travelling companions occupy. If you discover that one of your party is better placed than you, let him or her make the travel arrangements, book the taxi to the airport, decide what time to leave and what arrangements are to be made at your destination. In that way you can get into the slipstream of their energy to make this journey.

Another way to make a journey or business trip which appears in theory to be inauspicious is to change the route to build in some kind of dog-leg, if possible. This might mean a train journey or flight north-east, followed by a journey south-west which would still bring you to your destination. It may take you longer to work out and to get there, and may cost more, but you are not going into obvious or hidden danger.

14

FINDING OUT MORE

Practice

The best advice for you, having read this book, is to practise the various calculations covered in it. Practice will bring richness, questions and understanding of the system. One of the easiest tasks of this kind is to calculate the charts of family members or perhaps your colleagues at work. Try not to make them fit neatly into the descriptions that I have given, but rather look at the broad characteristics of Fire, Wood, Soil and so on. See if you can start to identify a pattern. To help you understand the various Houses through which we migrate on a yearly and monthly basis, make a list of key events in your life in recent years and notice what House you were in at the time. Again, see if a pattern emerges. Once you discover a pattern from your own experience it will help you predict months and years that are better suited for the activities that you have in mind.

Perhaps there are figures in history or modern life who particularly interest you. Obtain a biography or autobiography of that person and make a note of all the key dates in their life. See if there is a pattern. If so, try to relate this to their three numbers. Libraries and broadsheet newspapers are a good source of dates of birth and well-known anniversaries. Equally, they can provide you with a lot of questions.

I am always fascinated when I discover new astrological number 'twins' – for example, the possible similarity in the way professional colleagues regarded Margaret Thatcher and François Mitterrand (both 3.6.2). Another example is two of the most successful football managers of recent years – Bobby Robson and Kevin Keegan (4.8.1). What are the factors in common between Henry VIII and Robert Maxwell (5.7.3)? What about the fascinating connection between two of the key players responsible for the Charge of the Light Brigade in the Crimean War, Lord Raglan and the Earl of Cardigan (5.4.6)? There is also the extraordinary coincidence of two men born less than a month apart (both 9.5.9) who were responsible for inventing, respectively, the electric light bulb and the telephone – Thomas Edison (11 February 1847) and Alexander Graham Bell (2 March 1847). Both of them effectively had Fire highlighted in their chart. These examples are only the tip of the iceberg, and you will discover just as many coincidences when you begin to look at your own family and background.

Another useful way of practising and developing this system of astrology is to attend a seminar (see p.231).

Other Systems of Astrology

I am frequently asked how compatible this system is with other forms of astrology. The answer is that they are all compatible, but the danger lies when you try to mix up too many systems at once. Even to assume that this is the only form of astrology drawn from the *I Ching* is incorrect. The Flying Star astrology system is also based on the *I Ching*. The Tibetan 12 animals could also be used in combination with this system. No doubt there is a way of overlapping this system with Western astrology, whether Roman, Greek or Egyptian in origin. They all have something to offer. My advice to students on courses is to treat all this information with fresh eyes.

Confusion always arises when you try to make it fit with what you already know. Having little or no knowledge of astrology makes it far easier to understand this system, as you are not tempted to make it fit with some other system.

Over the past 20 years I have studied several facets of oriental philosophy and medicine, including astrology, Feng Shui, Shiatsu, acupressure and oriental diagnosis. While there are many different interpretations of these exciting subjects, ultimately you have to make your own choice and work with what resonates best with you. I was fortunate to have learnt from many oriental teachers who were plainly delighted by the prospect that a student would come up with new ideas and expressions of what they were teaching. I have attended countless discussions and debates on the meaning and compatibility of all these different systems. At the end of the day it is really down to our own judgement and what ultimately inspires us. I find it sad to hear the exasperated comments of students who have been 'told' first one thing and then another, and end up not knowing what to think. In some ways this is a reflection on Western studying methods: we are encouraged to take in knowledge and repeat it parrot fashion in some form of examination, rather than exploring issues and asking questions and forming our own opinions.

Final Word

9 Star Ki astrology offers you a new set of tools with which to map your life and negotiate the challenges that lie ahead, and I wish you every success in understanding and practising this system. I hope that it provides you with a new angle on relationships, on who you are, on who your colleagues are and, of course, on where you are. I also hope that for many of you this will be a stepping-stone towards looking at other facets of oriental culture that we in the West can develop and use to our advantage. Finally, I wish you health and peace.

REFERENCE/BIBLIOGRAPHY

Nine Star Ki, Michio Kushi (One Peaceful World Press, 1992)

An Anthology of I Ching, W.A. Sherrill & W.K. Chu (Arkana, 1989)

The Complete Guide to Nine Star Ki, Bob Sachs (Element, 1992)

The Ki, Takashi Yoshikawa (St Martin's Press, 1986)

The Nine Ki Handbook, S. Gagné & J. Mann (Spiralbound Books, 1985)

Feng Shui Made Easy, William Spear (Thorsons, 1995)

Feng Shui, Sarah Rossbach (Random House, 1984)

Creating Sacred Space with Feng Shui, Karen Kingston (Piatkus, 1996)

Principles of Feng Shui, Simon Brown (Thorsons, 1996)

Lao Tzu's Tao Te Ching, Timothy Freke (Piatkus, 1996)

The I Ching, Brian Browne Walker (Piatkus, 1996)

The I Ching, Richard Welhelm (Routledge & Kegan Paul, 1951)

WORKSHOPS, CONSULTATIONS AND HOROSCOPES

Workshops

I teach one and two day workshops on 9 Star Ki. For further information please contact:

United Kingdom
Feng Shui Network International
PO Box 2133, London W1A 1RL, England
Tel: +44 (0) 171 935 8935   Fax: +44 (0) 171 935 9295

Worldwide
Contact Jon Sandifer (see below)

Consultations and horoscopes

I conduct personal and business consultations which prove valuable in making decisions regarding work, travel and relationships.

I can also provide you with a personal horoscope based on 9 Star Ki astrology which will give you your own profile, where you are this year, which directions are most favourable for travel and major moves.

For further information please contact:

Jon Sandifer
PO Box 69
Teddington
Middx TW11 9SH

Telephone/Fax: +44 (0) 181 977 8988

e-mail: 106140.2645@Compuserve.COM

INDEX